EDUCATION IS NOT AN APP

While much has been written about the doors that technology can open for students, less has been said about its impact on teachers and professors. Although technology undoubtedly brings with it huge opportunities within higher education, there is also the fear that it will have a negative effect both on faculty and on teaching standards.

Education Is Not an App offers a bold and provocative analysis of the economic context within which educational technology is being implemented, not least the financial problems currently facing higher education institutions around the world. The book emphasizes the issue of control as being a key factor in whether educational technology is used for good or bad purposes, arguing that technology has great potential if placed in caring hands. While it is a guide to the newest developments in education technology, it is also a book for those faculty, technology professionals, and higher education policy-makers who want to understand the economic and pedagogical impact of technology on professors and students. It advocates a path into the future based on faculty autonomy, shared governance, and concentration on the university's traditional role of promoting the common good.

Offering the first critical, in-depth assessment of the political economy of education technology, this book will serve as an invaluable guide to concerned faculty, as well as to anyone with an interest in the future of higher education.

Jonathan A. Poritz is Associate Professor of Mathematics at Colorado State University-Pueblo, USA.

Jonathan Rees is Professor of History at Colorado State University-Pueblo, USA.

EDUCATION IS NOT AN APP

The future of university teaching in the Internet age

Jonathan A. Poritz and Jonathan Rees

Routledge
Taylor & Francis Group

LONDON AND NEW YORK

First published 2017
by Routledge
2 Park Square, Milton Park, Abingdon, Oxon OX14 4RN

and by Routledge
711 Third Avenue, New York, NY 10017

Routledge is an imprint of the Taylor & Francis Group, an informa business

© 2017 Jonathan A. Poritz and Jonathan Rees

British Library Cataloguing in Publication Data
A catalogue record for this book is available from the British Library

Library of Congress Cataloging in Publication Data
Names: Poritz, Jonathan Adam, 1964- author. | Rees, Jonathan, 1966- author.
Title: Education is not an app : the future of university teaching in the Internet age / Jonathan A. Poritz, Jonathan Rees.
Description: Abingdon, Oxon ; New York, NY : Routledge, 2017. | Includes bibliographical references and index.
Identifiers: LCCN 2016009927 |
ISBN 9781138910409 (hardback) | ISBN 9781138910416 (pbk.) |
ISBN 9781315693453 (ebook)
Subjects: LCSH: Higher education–Effect of technological innovations on. | Educational technology–Economic aspects. | Internet in higher education. | College teaching.
Classification: LCC LB2395.7 .P66 2017 | DDC 378.1/25–dc23
LC record available at https://lccn.loc.gov/2016009927

ISBN: 978-1-138-91040-9 (hbk)
ISBN: 978-1-138-91041-6 (pbk)
ISBN: 978-1-315-69345-3 (ebk)

Typeset in Bembo
by Cenveo Publisher Services
Printed in Great Britain by
Ashford Colour Press Ltd, Gosport, Hants

JP: I would like to dedicate this to Gabriel, Aiden, Raffaello, and Tristan (in merely chronological order), with whom I have seen the educational system from yet a third role, that of parent—which is sort of like the student role, but with the age and life experience (particularly since I am a professor) to be far more pissed off or abjectly grateful, on your behalf. Hopefully, this will also make me a more effective and empathetic teacher! Thanks to you four, and all my love.

JR: My greatest thanks go to the readers and commentators on my blog, More or Less Bunk [http://moreorlessbunk.net/blog]. Without you this book would not exist. Besides my co-author, my greatest influences with respect to the issues covered here have been Kate Bowles, Audrey Watters and Jim Groom. Thanks also to David Mazel, Ann Little, Bonnie Stewart and Jeremy Adelman. Special thanks to Routledge Editor Terry Clague who convinced me that writing a book based even partially upon a blog was actually a good idea.

CONTENTS

PREFACE

University professors are really busy people. We know this because we are both university professors—of math and history. Nevertheless, we have taken the time to follow developments in education technology because of its possible effects upon both of our fields, as well as upon faculty in general. Indeed, because of our particular interests—in computer science and the history of technology, respectively—we've followed these developments very closely. We have written this book so that our colleagues at universities around the world who haven't been following such developments can catch up. In the course of this long explanation, we've tried to analyze a fast-developing situation that should make university professors of all kinds very nervous.

Neither of us are anti-technology. We both believe that computers, the Internet, and Internet-related tools can help faculty do every aspect of their job (from teaching to research—even service!) better, and therefore serve as an enormous benefit to us and our students. However, the introduction of labor-saving technology into higher education is hardly a neutral act. The primary reason that we have written this book is our concern about who controls these technologies and how the introduction of such technologies will affect the distribution of power between faculty and administrators going forward.

Many of our sources for this analysis of education technology are in the higher education press, especially stories about how new programs are changing the way higher education operates on a day-to-day basis. On one level, many of these stories will be irrelevant by the time you read about them here. After all, the news is ephemeral almost by definition and many of these kinds of experiments are doomed to fail. However, on an abstract level, even failed experiments in higher education can tell us a lot about the power dynamics inside our institutions and this is the ultimate subject of this book. If faculty are not at the table for discussions about higher education technology, they risk being on the menu.

University professors are workers. New technologies have put the value of professors' skills at risk, just as they have for other workers in our changing economy. Nonetheless, we contend that faculty differ from other groups of workers in some important respects, and play a particular role in economy and society. Around one hundred years ago, the American Association of University Professors released an enormously influential statement (AAUP 1915) that included an explanation of

> the purposes for which universities exist. These are three in number:
>
> a. to promote inquiry and advance the sum of human knowledge;
> b. to provide general instruction to the students; and
> c. to develop experts for various branches of the public service.

While the mention of public service here may seem quaint in the current neoliberal moment, the assertion here that universities—and education, in general—help to shape the current and future zeitgeist is one that neoliberals and their opponents both accept (albeit some with dismay and others with approval). We might repurpose a famous quote (originally about writers and artists) by saying that *teachers are the engineers of human souls*. Probably, then, it makes sense to approach with great caution proposed radical transformations of the structures of universities and the jobs of their workers.

Radical transformation on the back of technological change does seem hard to avoid. Cheerleaders for this change point with derision to the "traditional" modes of teaching in which many professors have decades of experience: lectures, written examinations, chalkboards, office hours, and so on. But while technology offers a means to explore all kinds of new ways to teach old things, no method of pedagogy is necessarily bad simply because it's old and none is good simply because it's new. While university faculty can no longer reasonably expect to be the sole arbiters of success in their classrooms, the fact that the Internet exists is no excuse to destroy all of the traditional prerogatives that faculty have employed in their traditional classes since higher education began one or two thousand years ago (depending upon whether you start counting with the University of Bologna or Plato's Academy).

While these prerogatives are important, faculty should not have to enter a permanent state of class warfare with administrators in order to protect them because there are more than just two interest groups that will ultimately determine the outcome of this struggle. Students have an interest in a quality education. Whether that education includes educational technology, or not, depends upon the willingness of faculty to employ technological tools in their classes. It also depends upon the interests of thousands of companies based around the world that hope to profit by selling their educational technologies to universities. Particularly for those of us who work in state-run institutions, it also depends upon the wishes of the general public as expressed through their elected representatives.

This is why our approach to edtech issues is through the prism of political economy. Like it or not, your classroom is no longer entirely your own. A wide variety of interests are pressuring universities around the world to change the way education is conducted. Educational technology is a big part of that because of the effects its advocates say it has on both accountability and results. That's why this argument will eventually impact on your classroom, whether you actually use educational technology or not. Indeed, if you use tools like a learning management system or advising software it has affected your classroom already. So while you may be busy, you simply cannot afford to keep your head entirely in the sand with respect to edtech issues because how you do your job (and possibly your job itself) is at stake.

We work at the same university in Colorado, in the United States of America. Therefore, our reading material (like our perspective) is largely American in origin. Nonetheless, because of the global reach of neoliberalism and the historical accident that had the Internet invented in the U.S. and Silicon Valley located here, we believe that what happens in American higher education will not stay entirely within our borders. In other words, if you teach at a university outside the United States, you should read this book in order to see the kind of changes that are coming your way before they get there so that you can be prepared for them.

Of course, we don't think you have to be a college or university professor in order to benefit from, or enjoy, this book. Anyone who is concerned about the future of higher education in general should understand how the erosion of professorial prerogatives through technological change could destroy a system that has done a pretty good job for a very long time. Moreover, readers who are interested in making higher education better can look to this text for ways to improve education by empowering professors to do new things with new Internet-enabled tools.

The most important question that educational technology raises is not whether universities will employ it in the future. That ship has already sailed. Education technology will be a part of higher education moving forward, whether faculty like it or not. The most important issue that educational technology raises is who will ultimately control those technologies moving forward: faculty, administrators, or the companies that profit from the sale and use of those technologies. We think that struggle is just beginning and we have written this book to enlist as many interested people as possible around the world in the faculty's cause—that is, better education.

1

INTRODUCTION

False Flags

Google's business is not search. At least it is not directly search since Google doesn't charge for each of the several trillion search responses (Google, Inc. 2015) it gives to users each year. Nor is Facebook directly in the social media business, since it doesn't simply invoice its more than one billion users (Zuckerberg 2015) for helping them to talk to their friends online. Instead, these two companies have generated a combined market capitalization (in late 2015) of most of a trillion dollars (Yahoo Finance) by turning the questions users ask of the Internet, and their friendships, unfriendships, and snarky comments to each other, into a vast database of marketing research. In short, they are both in the advertising business.

As more and more education has been driven online, more pressure has been put on professors to flip, hybridize, automate, and/or MOOC[1] -ify their classes, it is appropriate to ask what are universities for? Is your university actually an institution of higher education? That is, is its highest priority the common good, built on the search for truth and its free expression? Or is it not really in the business that you thought it was?

By your university, we mean a college or university where you are faculty, staff, or a current or former student, or even one with which you simply have bonds of affection. If it is a private, for-profit institution, such as the University of Phoenix, DeVry University, one of the now-closed Corinthian Colleges, or any of the hundreds of other such schools, the answer is almost surely "no" as a matter of definition. A for-profit corporation's highest priority is the accumulation of profits, and it prioritizes the good of its shareholders over the common good—both as a matter of law, in fact.[2]

Non-profit institutions, both public and private, are at least freed from the gross profit motive in the construction of their identities. But other pressures, including financial, political, ideological, macro-economic, and demographic, can cloud our view of why universities exist. Nor can any explanation remain fixed and unchanging as the financial pressures on higher education mount and new pressures come into being. Just consider how fast the Internet has changed the world outside of academia already. The three-quarters of a trillion dollars of value in Google and Facebook stock did not even exist twenty years ago (apparently).

Our goal in this book is to explore how information technology (IT) has changed higher education (both for the better and for the worse) over the last twenty or twenty-five years. In the interest of transparency, we will not hide where we stand. Because we are both faculty members our interest is not merely in the financial viability of our employer, but much more in the health and sustainability of higher education as a whole, particularly its pedagogic and scholarly components. That's why we'll explore the impact of IT on universities from the perspective of the academic faculty. How can we use our experience and expertise to help make IT-related changes in universities benefit the real project of higher education, despite the ways that other forces (administrations, governing boards, politicians...) may seek to use IT as a weapon under some false flag or other (efficiency, student-centered, data-driven, anti-elitism, etc.)?

The title of this book is a metaphor from computer science. To explain, we have to look at the word *app*. This word was not widely used before 2010, when, however, it was voted *Word of the Year* by the American Dialect Society (ADS 2011). Rather computer users had the word *program*, as in *computer program*.

Perhaps what happened that year was simply that a faster, hipper generation wanted to talk and text about the *application programs*, or *applications*, which they loved, in contrast to the *systems software* (*software* being another fine synonym, though a mass noun, for *program*) such as the *operating systems*[3] and hardware drivers which they mostly took for granted.

In fact, *app* had been in use since the 1980s, but the massive usage change started around the time (and perhaps partly because) of Apple, Inc.'s ad campaign for its iPhone 3G with tag line "There's an app for that."[4] While the slogan inspired many amusing parodies, its serious purpose was to draw attention to the fact that the iPhone was not only a two-way radio with powerful sensors (GPS, camera, accelerometer, etc.) but also a *general-purpose computer*. Of course, preceding smartphones had also been *universal Turing machines* (UTMs)[5] but Apple was making the point that all of this computational power and flexibility was in the hands of everyone who had invested in an iPhone, available for the collective genius of all programmers to make of it a tool which would have uses in every corner of daily life.

Well, actually not *all* programmers. The day before the iPhone 3G was launched, Apple opened its App Store, and since then all programs which users want to run on their iPhones (also iPads and some other Apple devices) must come from the App Store. This is because the operating system for these devices, iOS, runs only *signed code*—programs which come with a piece of cryptographic metadata called a *digital signature*.[6] That is, unless you first *jailbreak* your phone, meaning that you or someone you hire (maybe in a dark alley, since the legality of jailbreaking has varied quite a bit with time and place) breaks the security of the iOS it is running to allow it to run even non–App Store software. (Note that while the legality of jailbreaking is a complex question, Apple declares that it voids the warranty since it is an explicit violation of the End User License Agreement (EULA), that multi-page document everyone pages through unread and clicks "OK" when activating a new device.)

As a consequence, anyone who wishes to sell or even to give away an app which will run under iOS, must register with Apple, pay for the iOS software development kit, submit their finished project for approval (not always granted, and sometimes rescinded for reasons which seem suspiciously like *Apple itself wants to make money that way*), and give Apple a portion of their sales—both up front, and for any sales made through in-app purchases—all in order to get Apple's digital signature on their app. iOS devices indeed implement universal Turing machines, but their universality is under the control of an Elder Sibling, not the actual owners of those devices.

There are certainly other software ecosystems than iOS[7] and we did skip over some important details in the iOS story above. Nevertheless, the word *app* exists solely to draw the distinction between two kinds of software: plain old *programs*, which presumably try to turn the power of that universal Turing machine in your pocket or on your desk into a tool that you control, and *apps*, which exist in a controlled and monitored environment and should not be expected to be free to do your bidding.

Apps are the serfs of the society of computer programs. Every time you ask for an app to perform a task (read a PDF, access your gradebook, etc.), you are saying you want to perform the task, but only in exactly the way predetermined and controlled by, and for the profit of, a third party who has interests aligned in a completely different direction from yours. This is not what we do in higher education; seek constrained truth for the advantage of specific powers that be. It is not something we should allow edtech in service of higher education to do, either.

Nothing Is Inevitable

Universities are always in a state of change. They build new buildings. They start new degree programs. They hire new presidents, who are often determined to make a permanent mark on a campus before moving on to greener pastures. What has really driven the recent spate of technologically-induced changes in American higher education has been fear of what Clayton M. Christensen of the Harvard Business School calls *disruption*. In 1997, Christensen wrote *The Innovator's Dilemma* (Christensen 2013), in which he described the process by which industry leaders were undercut by upstart firms in a wide range of industries.

In 2011, Christensen and his co-author, Henry J. Eyring, applied the same reasoning to higher education. "[T]he standard model has become unsustainable," they write in *The Innovative University* (Christensen and Eyring 2011). "To avoid disruption, institutions of higher education must develop strategies that transcend imitation. They must also master the disruptive technology of online learning and make other innovations." That argument has been picked up by technological enthusiasts of all kinds. In 2012, Sebastian Thrun, the founder of the MOOC purveyor Udacity famously told *WIRED* magazine (Leckart 2012) that "In 50 years ... there will be only 10 institutions in the world delivering higher education." Christensen, not to be outdone, predicted in 2013 (Suster 2013) that half of all American universities would go bankrupt in the next fifteen years.

Of course, Clayton Christensen was hardly the first observer to predict the imminent demise of higher education as we know it. "The collapse of higher education's business model has been predicted many times before," writes the higher education reporter Jeff Selingo in his 2013 book *College Unbound* (Selingo 2013), "Yet more colleges have opened their doors than closed them in the past 50 years." Indeed, by some measures—Nobel Prizes and patents but certainly not accessibility or affordability—the American system of higher education is the best in the world. If it can't survive the onslaught of new technology, what does this mean for higher education throughout the world?

What makes the American system of higher education particularly susceptible to disruption is not its weakness, but the strength of its opponents. Despite having experienced educational successes over more than a century, the United States is full of people who are opposed to the very idea of public education, or even public money going to subsidize education of any kind. Combine those opponents with the kinds of changes that the Internet has brought to other industries and the time appears to be ripe to cripple a successful system for no sin of its own. This does not mean that American higher education is perfect or that it and other systems around the world can't benefit from the kind of changes that technology can bring. However, to use it as an excuse to remove the good things while trying to fix the bad things would be the height of folly.

Online education is simply the newest weapon in a long series of attacks and it is hardly the one that does the most damage. (That might be the systematic defunding of American higher education which has been going on for decades now.) Online education is different because of the number of university faculty members who have happily agreed to participate in a practice which damages the institutions they love. Some of these faculty do so for the same reason that administrators and edtech startups do—to help themselves or their careers. Others who simply believe that the future is online are responding accordingly.

Will developments in Internet-based communications technology turn professors into the functional equivalent of ice-delivery men or travel agents? We do not know whether the Internet will make professors obsolete, but then again nobody else does, either. Yet this fact has not prevented the rise of a cottage industry of pundits who gleefully suggest that faculty in every department of the modern university are somehow heading for the scrap heap. Some of these pundits seem to welcome that possibility because they expect that the cost of a university education will decrease, with fewer professors collecting what they perceive to be hefty salaries, and they think that's good for society. Some of these people seem to welcome this possibility because they just hate university professors. We are perceived as elitists, and everybody likes to watch elitists get their comeuppance, except the elitists themselves.

As the 2012 saga surrounding the University of Virginia Board of Visitors' attempt to fire President Teresa Sullivan clearly demonstrated, faculty are capable of mounting fierce resistance to unwanted technological changes under the right circumstances. The emails leading up to Sullivan's initial firing demonstrate that UVa's Board of Visitors was steeped in press clippings that treated the transition to online education as an inevitability (Jaschik 2012). That attitude goes a long way toward explaining the Board's now legendary heavy-handedness: they wanted to ride the crest of a wave that supposedly well-informed people were all telling them is already coming.

For technology companies that stand to profit by disrupting higher education, treating the transition to an online future as a *fait accompli* serves as a very effective business strategy. By continually reinforcing the idea that traditional higher education is way behind the times, they gather public support for costly online initiatives that might not otherwise go forward. Education reformers have been looking for ways to replace teachers with *teaching machines* for almost a century now (Ferster 2014). The opportunity to restructure universities around the Internet might prove irresistible to even the most traditional administrators.

Equally importantly, the rhetoric of higher education's inevitable decline infects faculty with a sense of learned helplessness. Why try to fight the inevitable when we have so much else to worry about in our busy lives already? (Because the fidelity of higher education to its true mission and the professional lives of countless university employees are at stake.) Leave educational technology to the private, for-profit companies and your university administrators and many faculty may very well not like the results because faculty and students have different interests from administrators and edtech companies.

Ever since the 1970s, the ranks of the professoriate have been increasingly occupied by adjuncts, faculty with no job security, given few (if any) benefits and earning as little as a few thousand dollars for each course they teach. According to the American Association of University Professors (AAUP), the longest-active and most successful organization dedicated to the health of higher education and the working conditions of faculty in modern history, more than 50 percent of professors today work only part-time (despite teaching the equivalent of a full-time course load) and 76 percent of all faculty work off the tenure track (AAUP 2014). While we certainly recognize that some administrators care about the quality of the education that their universities provide, the widespread use of adjunct faculty suggests that monetary concerns trump discussions of quality. This is not to suggest that adjunct faculty are inferior teachers by definition, but anybody who has to worry about putting food on the table, or has to commute long distances between campuses to make a wage on which they can barely get by, will have a difficult time giving their students all the attention that they deserve.

Certainly, the subject of adjuncts is a book by itself. When you consider the possible effects of educational technology on classroom teaching and you wonder why professors in the United States don't do more to maintain control over their own classrooms, you should remember that 76 percent figure because we aren't going to repeat it in every single chapter. However, with respect to the intentions of administrators towards faculty, the important thing about those adjunct faculty members is that their presence is an effect of the same forces that make edtech so dangerous to tenure-track faculty. Only 24 percent of university presidents who responded to a 2011 Pew survey said that they would like most faculty members at their institutions to be full-time and tenured (Taylor et al. 2011). While adjunct faculty have been around since the early 1970s, the current state of educational technology makes the all-adjunct university more possible than ever before. Any administrator willing to replace traditional faculty with adjuncts is probably willing to replace faculty altogether.[8]

The notion that many university administrators who don't care very much about educational quality would like to replace full-time, tenured faculty with technology should not be controversial. After all, technology does not require a salary. Technology will not talk back at meetings. Technology does not demand a say in running the university. Even if that educational technology requires humans to run it, the deskilling associated with this "tsunami" will allow universities easily to replace trained professors with less-skilled machine tenders. Because those machine tenders can, in theory, be drawn from anywhere on the planet with an Internet connection, their wages will inevitably be much lower than the tenured professors laboring at any school's physical campus. As long as students are willing to pay for tuition in exchange for this kind of education, there will be administrators willing to provide it.

We are not alleging a conspiracy here. We don't think that America's university presidents are all meeting at palatial retreats where they quietly plot the destruction of the professoriate as we know it. What we do believe is that there is plenty of evidence that many people with power over edtech choices, acting independently, have come to the conclusion that faculty power should be stripped, their livelihoods destroyed, and the educational consequences ignored.

Universities and the people who run them are responding to a set of pressures, particularly cost pressures—the same kinds of pressures that gave rise to the use of adjunct faculty during the early 1970s. For example, symbolizing the political pressure on presidents to cut costs, California Governor Jerry Brown has called for the University of California system to develop courses that do not require human intervention (Koseff 2014). For every president or politician willing to express this goal in public, there are probably ten more who are thinking it, but who are too scared to say so publicly—yet. As a result of these pressures, a future without any professors at all has become part of what technologists refer to as the *adjacent possible*, something that is technologically feasible but not quite here yet.

In response to these same pressures, too many faculty have chosen to defer to what they see as the inevitability of our online future. "[D]o I like online courses?" asked one faculty member in the pages of the *Chronicle of Higher Education*. "My answer is that it doesn't matter. The students like them, and we have to adjust to their demands" (Hartz 2012). To us, this kind of passive acceptance of the future is very unprofessorial. How do we know that students like online education, let alone demand it? Assuming they do, why should we listen to them? After all, if all of our students demanded "A"s without any work, would we give in to that demand even though it would harm their education? More importantly, shouldn't we all, as scholars, try to understand all the factors that influence the course that our institutions will take in the future?

While many people who are interested in computers and the Internet have written books about the glorious future that computers offer students, to our knowledge nobody has written about the effects of technology upon teachers and professors. We fear the effects of these changes upon faculty like ourselves. We also fear the effects of these changes upon students as the quality of education will inevitably suffer as a result. We offer this book as inspiration to get concerned faculty and other friends of education to organize and do something about these developments before it's too late. If we do nothing, the technological processes that have changed other social systems might affect education in the same way.

Autonomy and agency are paramount goals we have for our students in higher education, and we cannot achieve these goals by carelessly imposing restrictive technological infrastructures, installing apps in students' heads. Nor can we be successful if we do not model autonomy and agency during our own lives in the university environment, if we let administrators and bureaucratic structures install apps on us and in our classrooms.

This essential distinction will infuse every section of this book. "When rightly used," argued Gustav Stickley, the founder of the Arts and Crafts Movement in the early twentieth century, "the machine is simply a tool in the hands of a skilled worker" (Pollan 2013, quoting Stickley). When control over technology is placed in caring hands, great things can happen. When the quality of classroom instruction is sacrificed for the sake of expediency, market ideology or cost, the result will be disastrous for nearly everyone involved, except the administrators and Silicon Valley denizens who convinced universities to adapt it in the first place. On the contrary, we believe that every student, in person or online, deserves a caring teacher committed to their personal achievement in higher education, and this impersonal, neoliberal attitude towards learning ignores this basic right.

When it comes to educational technology, nothing is inevitable. There are many different kinds of educational technology. Even if technology will definitely play a bigger role in higher education in the future, there are still plenty of different scenarios under which that future can play out. The goal of university professors should be to make sure that their voices, as well as their expertise, determine exactly how the Internet will influence higher education going forward. We hope this book offers faculty (as well as other interested, education-friendly observers) all the information they need in order to understand how edtech may affect college and university teaching in the future.

A Matter of Trust

Again, none of this means that we are anti-technology. Indeed, both of us are deeply interested in technological tools that can help us teach our respective classes (mathematics/computer science and history) better. However, even the best educational tools can become weapons when wielded by the wrong hands for the wrong reason. For example, the anthropologist turned edtech entrepreneur Marie Norman "spoke with an administrator at a university that has steered hard in the direction of publisher-created online courses. He sneered at my company's faculty-driven approach to course creation, maintaining that faculty ownership of courses is a thing of the past" (Norman 2014). That's a problem because a lot of administrators don't know what to do with online courses once they have them. For example, the University of California system spent $4.3 million to get students from around the world to sign up for their online courses. Only one student did so (Asimov 2013).

Unfortunately, too many professors have responded to this kind of expensive technological utopianism by deferring to administrative initiatives no matter how unwise they happen to be. We think tools like lecture capture and other edtech developments over recent years offer exciting new classroom possibilities, but only when faculty themselves have the greatest say over how those tools get used and even what tools get used in the first place.

If you teach at a university where you trust your administrators to make the right decisions with respect to educational technology, then you are very lucky. The chances are, you have a full-time, tenure-track appointment at a college or university that can afford to experiment with the latest technology and is not cash-strapped. This is not true of most American professors at most American universities. Public universities across the United States are under enormous pressure to cut costs at precisely the time that non-educational costs (like athletics or supporting an ever-increasing army of middle-managers) are expanding. Unscrupulous private companies sometimes present their product as a magic bullet to save labor costs so that these other expenses can continue unabated. Other educators work at private for-profit colleges and universities, where financial concerns are literally at the center of their school's very existence. Even community colleges, the largest and fastest-growing sector of American higher education today, still face pressures to expand their size to capture the most potential students at a time when their services are increasingly sought by workers who desire the retraining they need to get ahead.

Or perhaps you don't teach in the United States at all. The United States has had a system of higher education which has, at times, served as a model for other countries (see the history in Goldin and Katz (2009)). Even today, it attracts students from all over the world, and many universities do an excellent job of helping motivated (and financially able, we must admit) students change the courses of their lives. It also goes without saying that universities in the U.S. produce enormous quantities of truly ground-breaking research. For this reason, we remain astounded that so many people want to disrupt American higher education.

Using the Internet as a way to pull up the existing system, root and branch, and then replace it with a brand new species, strikes us as absurd. Therefore, we offer this mostly-American rundown of the effects of educational technology on the practice of university teaching as a cautionary tale for faculty around the world. After all, ill-winds blowing in the American higher education like the casualization of employment and significantly decreased public support are also blowing in many other countries. Why would anyone think that the misuse of educational technology would be any different? (Indeed, some technologies, like MOOCs, are explicitly designed from their very inception to transform education around the world.)

What separates educational technology from these other problems is that it can be a force for good as well as evil. That's why we believe that every student, whether online or in a face-to-face classroom, deserves a caring instructor dedicated to helping them learn. As long as technology does not disrupt or harm that relationship in any way, we support it. In fact, if you use the right educational technologies in the right ways then your university will become better than it has ever been before. But how can you tell a good technology from a bad technology—or more subtly, from a good technology that's being used badly? You have to understand the political and economic context in which that technology is being introduced.

Politicians, educational technology companies, administrators: these are the people who hold the power to take even the best educational technologies and turn them into a faculty member's worst nightmare. Whether MOOCs or Learning Management Systems (LMSs), these technologies are being marketed primarily as ways to keep costs down, rather than as tools to improve educational quality. All of these technologies, along with many others that will be discussed in this book, maintain a patina of respectability because they can be used as effective educational tools when placed in the right hands for the right reasons. Additionally, the forces behind their adoption can argue that they should be adopted on behalf of students, especially because they present the possibility of driving tuition fees down. Unfortunately, the responsible employment of these technologies seems unlikely because of the way that universities are financed. In other words, educational technology has its own political economy which too many of its advocates completely ignore.

This book is about the economic context into which educational technology is being inserted. In other words, we want to examine the relationship between which technologies get selected by universities and the general financial problems of higher education almost everywhere. We will make an extended argument about under what circumstances educational technology can be used for good purposes, and under what purposes it is likely to be used for bad ones. But here's a good rule of thumb for all such situations: trust faculty to employ technology well whenever they have the power to bend that technology into the way they teach already. Don't create a whole new technologically-infused learning system when the old one works just fine. Trust the market to do what's right for education and you'll have no idea what the result will be, other than it will probably be right for the market.

Unlike most (but by no means all) of the writers we've read on this subject, we understand the labor system into which new technologies are being introduced, as well as the scientific details of these technologies.[9] With the constant talk of gloom and doom for higher education, you don't have to be an adjunct faculty member to fear for your job anymore. But even faculty members who aren't in a privileged tenure-track position still have some power by being the ones on the ground in the classroom (or on the Internet in an online classroom) where the success or failure of any particular technology will ultimately be determined. Change may be inevitable but faculty members are not helpless. Indeed, we think they possess an extraordinary amount of power to determine what kinds of educational technology will survive their infancy. This book is designed to help faculty exercise that power in ways that aren't just best for themselves, but in ways that are best for education in general.

Notes

1 A *MOOC* is a *massive, open, on-line course*. MOOCs are the subject of Chapter 3.
2 Although the relevant law is quite complex. See Milton Friedman's famous essay (Friedman 1970), or a more nuanced view in Stout (2008) and in the references contained therein.
3 An *operating system* is a program which manages the interactions of running programs and their access to basic system resources. Examples are iOS, Android, Windows, OS X, and GNU/Linux.
4 Slogan (™) Apple, Inc.
5 Alan Turing, the British mathematician who invented computer science and single-handedly had an enormous effect on the outcome of WWII by directing the work of breaking German military codes, defined what is now called a *universal Turing machine:* very roughly, a device capable of performing any computation which can be clearly stated as an algorithm.
6 A *digital signature* on data is generated by applying a mathematical algorithm to the data and the signer's cryptographic key. Anyone can *verify* the signature to check if (a) the data are unchanged; and (b) the signature was created by someone with access to the signer's key.
7 For example, matters are somewhat different—and freer—for Android phones. On the desktop, the operating systems tend not to require signed code, but often a cloud-based service or piece of locally installed software subject to detailed contractual restrictions will be as closed-down as any app on iOS.
8 Ironically, since adjunct faculty are easier to replace than tenure-track professors, they will likely feel the effects of automated education first.
9 We also have some understanding of relevant legal questions, which will be quite important in Chapters 4 and 8. But we are not lawyers, so please do not take anything in this book as legal advice.

2

ONLINE EDUCATION

The Good, the Bad, and the Ugly

Conflicting Priorities

Speaking at Oxford University in 2000, former Princeton University President William Bowen was skeptical about the advantages of online education, calling these efforts both "promising and risky." With respect to the future, he declared that,

> as far ahead as any of us can see... there will be a demand for an education at both undergraduate and graduate levels that continues to emphasize the informal as well as the formal modes of learning that are possible in a collegiate setting.
>
> *(Bowen 2001)*

Speaking at Stanford in 2012, Bowen's skepticism about online education had disappeared. "I am today a convert," he told the crowd at the campus that made Silicon Valley possible.

> Far greater access to the Internet, improvements in Internet speed, reductions in storage costs, the proliferation of increasingly sophisticated mobile devices, and other advances have combined with changing mindsets to suggest that online learning, in many of its manifestations, can lead to at least comparable learning outcomes relative to face-to-face instruction at a lower cost.
>
> *(Bowen 2015a)*

Notice his simultaneous emphasis on both costs and the quality of instruction. His skepticism disappeared over that twelve-year gap because of improvements on both fronts. It also helped that Ithaka, which employs Bowen these days, had come out with a single idiosyncratic study suggesting that the results of online and face-to-face classes were comparable. That result has yet to be duplicated adequately to make such sweeping generalizations. Nevertheless, Bowen is now ready to proceed as fast as possible (Watters and Goldrick-Rab 2015).

So too are presidents at countless universities across the United States. You can see why simply by examining the ever-increasing number of students who are now taking online courses. As of the fall of 2012, approximately a quarter of all undergraduates took at least one online course (and that number has only grown since then) (Shirky 2015). Online education is not going away. Indeed, the more it grows, the greater the impact it will be likely to have on the way that all university classes are conducted.

The nature of that impact depends upon the quality of these courses. Certainly, the quality of at least some online instruction has gotten better since this kind of education debuted back in the late-1990s. Professors can do amazing things in an online setting that simply can't be done in a conventional classroom. It is now possible to employ all sorts of useful technological tools online that simply weren't available back then—even for courses where faculty members still meet in the same room during regular class periods.

However, it is also indisputable that at least some of the online courses offered at American universities today are pretty awful. Many schools—especially for-profit, exclusively online schools—create cookie-cutter classes designed to entice as many students as possible and staff them with exclusively adjunct faculty. This is their business model. We would suggest that the best way to make sure that universities offer more of the good courses and fewer of the bad ones is for the faculty to be directly involved in the planning and implementation of all online courses. The more input faculty have with respect to online classes going forward, the better those online classes will eventually be.

That's because many administrators are operating under a different set of priorities than faculty are. In a traditional face-to-face university, the professors and students meet on campus. Tuition is exchanged for instruction, while services, like room and board, are paid for with other fees. In an online class, the pool of potential professors and students expands to any qualified person with an Internet connection. "Online education has freed us from the limited pool of professors in a local area," explained the co-founder and CEO of a company called Professors on Demand in a 2013 press release entitled *Centenary College Sponsors New Online Global Database of Professors for Online Education* (PRN 2013). Based solely on the law of supply and demand, having more workers able to bid for a job will make it possible for employers to decrease what they decide to pay the winners.

This same freedom from a limited pool of professors makes it possible for universities with online programs to draw upon a practically infinite supply of students. Theoretically, they could even discount tuition fees for online courses and still make more money if the total number of students enrolled increases enough in response. The problem is that the more students there are in an online program, the less likely it becomes that any one of them will get the kind of face-to-face attention available in an on-campus setting. This is the first step down the road to the fantasy of profit without workers, and the more technologically sophisticated that online courses get the more possible that fantasy becomes.

"We can already, today, replicate much of what colleges are charging a great deal of money for and distribute that information electronically at almost no marginal cost," writes Kevin Carey (Carey 2015). However, the distribution of information is not the same as education, but if this definition takes hold there will be nothing to prevent universities from essentially minting money. With no new buildings to pay for, or heat, during the wintertime, administrations have only to pay for the IT infrastructure needed to make giant online classes possible. Only the influence of concerned faculty and the willingness of students to participate in these arrangements can prevent this future from taking hold.

Nobody expects university administrators to admit that they see online courses only as a way to save money and that they don't care about the consequences for quality. Indeed, few of them will admit that they don't think that online education saves money at all. If it did, why don't they pass those savings on to students in the form of lower tuition fees? Probably because they see those savings as subsidizing other parts of the university. "It is a great opportunity, we think, for enhancing learning and shedding costs," explained an Executive Assistant to the President of California State University–Fullerton, which is part of a system that was hit particularly hard by state budget cuts in 2012 (Moran 2012). But what if it does neither?

Unfortunately, as Janet Napolitano, the President of the University of California system noted in early 2014, online education is "harder than it looks and if you do it right, it doesn't save all that much money" (Bernstein 2014). Design an online program badly and it becomes even less likely that a university will make any money educating students this way. When the state of Florida decided it wanted to start an entirely online university quickly, it contracted with Pearson to do it for them. That agreement allowed Pearson to keep 60 percent of the tuition money from every student who signed up, whether that company managed to meet its recruitment targets or not (Simon 2015).

Even when a university system doesn't rely on expensive private contractors to establish its online programs, high start-up costs and the persistence of forces (like professors) pressing for maintaining educational quality in online settings will be likely to keep costs high. For example, studies have shown that the best kind of online education is the blended model because its combination of online and face-to-face instruction does the most to promote learning (Enyedy 2014, 13). Unfortunately, this model has all of the high start-up costs that an entirely online curriculum does and few of the cost savings, since buildings still need to be maintained and local faculty paid. Will interested faculty have the opportunity to teach this kind of expensive classes if they see fit? A look at the origins of online education suggests that the answer to that question will often be "no."

Doing It Wrong

Online education as we know it today began in the late-1990s. An all-online model originated with for-profit institutions that hoped to pass on the profits, due to expected cost savings of their new manner of instruction, to their stockholders.

Emulating this model, a wide variety of non-profit, especially public, universities have tried to overload those classes with additional students, thereby destroying the possibility of close contact between students and professors (Peekhaus 2014). This, to borrow Napolitano's phrase, is not "doing it right," but in today's environment of educational austerity, too many administrators are willing to do it wrong.

Early online efforts, both for-profit and not, turned out the same way, as the late historian David Noble related in a series of web articles, followed by a path-breaking 2001 book entitled *Digital Diploma Mills*, having little in the way of quality control. His critique still has much to teach us. As Noble explained,

> Promoters of instructional technology and 'distance learning' advanced with ideological bravado as well as institutional power, the momentum of human progress allegedly behind them. They had merely to proclaim 'it's the future' to throw skeptics on the defensive and convince seasoned educators that they belonged in the dustbin of history.

These tactics have the explicit effect of limiting debate—convincing faculty that it's the promoters' version of online education or nothing and trying to limit the role of faculty in shaping the exact nature of that future. "The monotonal mantras about our inevitable wired destiny," Noble wrote,

> the prepackaged palaver of silicon snake-oil salesmen, echoed through the halls of academe, replete with sophomoric allusions to historical precedent (the invention of writing and the printing press) and sound bites about the imminent demise of the 'sage on the stage' and 'bricks and mortar institutions'.
> *(Noble 2002, 50)*

The language is so fresh it's amazing to think that Noble first wrote these words in the late-1990s.

Noble also understood the effect of such schemes on faculty better than most do fifteen years later. "The commodification of education requires the interruption of this fundamental educational process and the disintegration and distillation of the educational process into discrete, reified, and ultimately saleable things or packages of things." Break down the process of teaching into discrete bites, and it will be much harder for teachers to make a living. "In the wake of this transformation," Noble explained,

> teachers become commodity producers and deliverers, subjects of the familiar regime of commodity production in any other industry, and students become consumers of yet more commodities. The relationship between teacher and student is thus reestablished, in an alienated mode, through the medium of the market, and the buying and selling of commodities takes on the appearance of education. But it is, in reality, only a shadow of education, an assemblage of pieces without the whole.
> *(Noble 2002, 3–4)*

It's education as capitalist accumulation, all enabled by technology.

The key to making this reality possible is to automate as much of the teaching process as possible. The managerial class will inform the faculty that they do this so that they can spend more time doing the kind of personalized instruction that really counts, but that assumes that they are not replaced entirely. As the technology critic Nick Carr has explained, "The dream that the technologies of automation will liberate us from work, the dream expressed by McLuhan, is a seductive one....The emancipatory power would be released only through political, economic, and social changes. Technology would always serve its master" (Carr 2015). For example, developing and teaching an online course requires more professorial hours than regular ones (Freeman 2015). However, with the second and third times, online and face-to-face courses take about the same number of hours both to teach and develop. What's important to remember about these results is that they are dependent upon the content of the course not changing. In other words, the online education machine begins to go itself. If you want to change content, that requires more work and more pay. How can any faculty member be sure their administration will let them? Indeed, if the machine can go by itself while under faculty control, that raises the possibility for the future that the machine could go by itself without any faculty input whatsoever.

While professors will no doubt object to the idea that they should be, or even can be, replaced by computer programs, whether they have the power to object is another question worth asking. Shared governance is the idea that faculty should have an important role—the lead role, if possible—in determining the university decisions related to its educational and research missions because they are the experts on these areas on campus. Because of its technical nature and the economies of scale that online education offers, its mere existence threatens shared governance as it has been practiced in American higher education over the last hundred years. Ultimately, the survival of shared governance in the Internet Age depends upon any university's unwillingness to sacrifice educational quality upon the altar of efficiency.

Uncertainty about the survival of shared governance has encouraged the rise of a cottage industry of pundits, who gleefully suggest that faculty in every department of the modern university are somehow heading for the scrap heap. In a recent survey conducted by the Pew Internet and American Life Project and Elon University's Imaging the Internet Center, 60 percent of these people agreed that, "By 2020, higher education will be quite different from the way it is today. There will be mass adoption of teleconferencing and distance learning to leverage expert resources" (Anderson, et al. 2012). Indeed, the huge amount of Silicon Valley venture capital money invested in educational start-ups is both a testament to the faith that investors have in the power of technology to change American universities and a huge force to make change happen.

Anyone actually acquainted with higher education can easily imagine how the future could turn out differently than most pundits expect. One possibility would be a future where students take some but not all of their classes online. This would allow them to take advantage of the convenience that online education can offer, but still get the benefits of face-to-face contact for all the courses where that contact matters most—perhaps in their majors—while they might reserve their online classes for their general education requirements. Indeed, having the instructor of their online classes on campus offers a substantial advantage (particularly if something goes wrong with the technology) over taking an entirely online course with someone on the other side of the planet.

Another possible problem with the future of online classes as Internet experts see them would be their failure to satisfy their most important constituencies. For example, if students chose to forgo university rather than take all their classes online then the most effective educational technology in the world won't be able to help them. Staring at a computer screen for hours on end can be difficult—even dehumanizing—especially if people don't get to choose what they're doing online. If students resent being treated like a number in large classes already, taking online classes that might teach thousands of people at a time would only make that problem worse. If learning online becomes their only option, they might begin to listen to a growing chorus of higher education critics trying to convince them to skip university altogether.

Few schools discount tuition fees for their online classes since they want to keep the cost savings that online education makes possible entirely for themselves. Because the tuition fees that schools charge for taking online classes are generally as expensive (or in the case of for-profit schools, even more expensive) than on-campus learning, online education also needs to satisfy student loan providers who make it possible for so many students to attend university in the first place.

In the United States, the government is everyone's loan provider of first resort, since their interest rates are usually lower than those of private providers. However, the government's rates are already going up thanks to austerity policies in the federal budget. In the future, that same austerity will be likely to decrease the entire pool of available government loan money. With a shrinking pool of money available, sending loan dollars to an unproven educational method rather than a proven one makes little economic sense. Everybody complains that university is expensive, yet countless studies demonstrate that higher education is still valuable even if it's not necessarily as valuable as it once was (Cassidy 2015). That makes lending to university students a good risk, especially since those loans aren't dischargeable in a bankruptcy court.

Changing the way that education is delivered entails risk. While proponents of online education like to point out that universities haven't changed the way they operate for several centuries, introducing values that demand constant change is not necessarily conducive to education of any kind. Good educational technology can be extremely expensive, but if universities use revenue from online education as a way to backfill cuts in state aid or for other non-educational purposes, the quality of the education they provide will inevitably suffer.

This is where the voices of professors could make a difference, but one of the many reasons why online education saves money for schools is that they can farm those classes out to poorly paid adjuncts who must remain voiceless to keep their jobs. If those adjuncts need to teach multiple sections to make ends meet, the quality of their teaching will inevitably suffer. Adjuncts are also more likely to have jobs that depend entirely upon their continued ability to put butts in seats and making classes easy is the easiest way to keep getting students online, or otherwise.

If what students actually learn in university means something for employment purposes, then processes like dumbing down courses or just being overly solicitous of students in order to get tuition revenue will destroy the economic foundation of higher education by encouraging students, lenders, and employers alike to back away. While many informed observers think that a mass move towards online learning is inevitable, nobody seems prepared to cope with the fallout if this all turns out to be a passing fad. The financial costs of this current craze are already staggering, whether it lasts into the long term or not. The human costs of failure on students and professors alike have yet to be felt, but they have the potential to be just as high. The key is to go online while still maintaining quality. Unfortunately, the fact is that online classes create new problems that simply don't exist in the face-to-face world.

For example, when you host an online course on someone else's platform, your course isn't really yours. Professor Jennifer Ebbeler learned this the hard way when she wrote an online version of the Roman History course for her home department, Classics, at the University of Texas – Austin. After two years of work, her department replaced the lecturer who had built the course with her as the lead instructor going forward. Professor Ebbeler felt the replacement was unqualified. "They think it doesn't matter who they put in charge because the course will teach itself," she told the *Chronicle of Higher Education*. "And yet I've been clear all along that that's not the case" (Kolowich 2015). Imagine for a moment, a department pulling the same trick with a face-to-face course. Getting her lecture notes from her would be hard enough, let alone the rest of the materials and knowledge that make the class a class. However, Ebbeler poured much of her knowledge into the course's design, which gave her department enough control to determine exactly who teaches it, whether she likes it or not.

Yet things could have gone worse, with respect to administrative interference in online courses. In the late-1990s, David Noble explicitly worried that once faculty committed their courses to computer programs, they (like the hero in Kurt Vonnegut's novel *Player Piano*) could be replaced by themselves—or at least a close facsimile of the professors that they used to be. Fortunately, to this point in the development of online education, faculty members are more important than ever. After all, somebody has to supervise the work of students who not only need to learn the material, but who also need to know all the technological skills necessary for them to access that material.

Moving to a totally online format also changes the nature of the work that any professor can assign to their students. For example, history professors who are interested in teaching their students specific historical facts have no idea whether their students have learned them or simply Googled them. Math professors have no way of knowing whether their students are actually doing basic arithmetic or using a calculator——or even if they are integrating a complicated function with their bare brains or simply copying the answer down from wolframalpha.com, a site which (for free) can do almost all of the straight calculations in the standard undergraduate mathematics curriculum. These problems are the effects of students being able to do their work without being observed.

Another possible ill effect of an entirely online educational environment is the likelihood that students will open another tab while listening to an online lecture (or some other relevant content-related activity) and check their Facebook accounts. To be fair, plenty of students do something similar now in their face-to-face classes, but the absolute certainty that they could not get caught makes it logical to assume that the problem would get worse.

On a closely related note, cheating is another problem with online education from its early days that remains important today. If you can't see the student at the other end of the computer screen it is very difficult to know if they are actually the person who they say they are. To paraphrase a classic *New Yorker* cartoon, in online education, nobody knows you're a dog. It is not hard to Google up sites where people offer to take entire online courses for you if the price is right. After all, how will anybody know? Any student feckless enough to employ the better-known services of people who write entire papers from scratch for them is fully capable of outsourcing an entire course, if they think they can get away with it. Given the gold-rush mentality of most schools with online branches, they probably can.

Solving the problems associated with identifying students online presents another set of problems involving privacy. Basically, guaranteeing that nobody in an online class cheats requires setting up a miniature police state that affects every student in a class. The situation at Rutgers University in early 2015, as described in a campus newspaper there, suggests the extremes needed to solve online education's security problem:

> Are you planning on taking an online course at Rutgers next semester? Then you might need to download University-sanctioned software that will track your facial identity, photo ID and browser activity...Rutgers University has implemented a recognition suite called ProctorTrack for online courses. ProctorTrack records face, knuckle and personal identification details during online courses. [A local reporter] also notes that the system 'keeps track of all activity in the monitor, browser, webcam and microphone' throughout each session.
>
> *(Whythe 2015)*

It should go without saying that no such measures are required for face-to-face classes since the professor can provide test security simply by being present during exams.

Ironically, it is the most convenient aspect of online education, the flexibility to take classes at any time, that makes proctoring them so difficult. The physical separation between students and teachers breeds the security problems that these draconian measures are supposed to solve. Advocates for online education seldom consider this particular cost, but as such courses grow more popular more of such measures will be increasingly necessary. Whether the benefits are worth such costs is for both students and administrators to decide. What is best for assuring the quality of an online education might not be best for minimizing the cost of the project.

The importance of this balancing act makes the role of faculty as arbiters of educational quality so important in an online environment. If universities were to look to faculty for guidance when trying to resolve these kinds of problems, they could gain the insight of people who have years of teaching experience—sometimes in both face-to-face and online settings. Yes, few faculty are taught how to teach in graduate school, but there is such a thing as learning by doing. Professional teachers are the best judges of whether any particular online arrangement meets the standards of quality needed in any particular discipline.

Faculty members know what content has to be covered. They know what skills their students should learn from their disciplines. Even online, they are in the best position to observe student learning—especially with respect to intangible qualities such as writing, critical thinking, and problem-solving skills which cannot be measured through multiple-choice assessment techniques. Any online environment that stifles the traditional prerogatives that face-to-face educators can exercise is not just a threat to the quality of the education that those professors can provide, it is a threat to their academic freedom.

Enter the Disruptors

Some pundits seem to welcome the possibility that professors will disappear entirely in the new technologically-driven higher educational future because they expect that the cost of a university education will decrease, with fewer professors collecting what they perceive to be hefty salaries, and they think that's good for society. Some of these people seem to welcome the possibility because they just hate university professors. We are perceived as elitists, and everybody likes to watch elitists get their comeuppance, except the elitists themselves. Even if faculty tried to justify their existence by explaining carefully how they make the university experience better, students would be likely to go for the cheap, online automated alternative because the forces of the market would leave them no other choice.

But in all this talk about whether the Internet will eventually force professors to go the way of the dodo, few people ask whether professors **should** vanish from this Earth. What if the future of higher education isn't entirely online? What if the presence of a human being in a physical classroom teaching them is essential to learning for psychological if not pedagogical reasons? While such questions may seem crazy, conventional wisdom is sometimes wrong. After all, a lot of experts once believed that the Sun revolves around the Earth, that Saddam Hussein had weapons of mass destruction, and that the value of real estate in the United States only goes up. The Internet stock bubble of the late-1990s should by itself give pause to anyone who believes that venture capitalists can predict the future.

Unfortunately, a large number of interests are lined up to interfere in the free exercise of faculty prerogatives so that they can make a professor-less future more of a reality. The most obvious of these forces are certain university administrators. As Carnegie Mellon University President Subra Suresh told the Global Learning Council, "the French politician Georges Clemenceau once said that, 'War is too important to be left to the generals.' Some would argue learning is too important to be left to professors and teachers." (Williams 2014). That's really an amazing statement when you think about it. After all, the job of professors and teachers is to facilitate learning, while administrators like Suresh have so much else to do.

One of these administrative functions is to decide where the money that any university has is going to be spent. Even when some expenditure is undertaken with consultation from representative faculty bodies, no professor has time to track everything. This makes it possible for administrators who want to take more of the classes at their universities online to do precisely that, whether the regular faculty there accedes to that desire or not. Labor historians like to refer to "control of the shop floor" when considering struggles between workers and their employers during the late nineteenth and early twentieth centuries when industrialization was still new. The Internet makes it possible for employers to start an entirely new factory with new rules and new standards. With respect to higher education, whether those new rules and standards are good for students remains open to question.

Of course, making sure that professors do their jobs is another of the functions of university administration, but the advent of online education (as well as online components of traditional face-to-face education) opens up countless new areas for oversight. When all communication between professors and their students takes place online, every aspect of a class can be monitored. "Once faculty and courses go online," wrote David Noble in *Digital Diploma Mills*, "administrators gain much greater direct control over faculty performance and course content than ever before and the potential for administrative scrutiny, supervision, regimentation, discipline and even censorship increase[s] dramatically" (Noble 2002, 32). Having someone watch every exchange between professors and their students is no longer necessary since the use of the same *big data* techniques that Facebook or the National Security Agency uses in its monitoring of Internet activity becomes a possibility inside universities for the first time.

Ironically, this kind of monitoring will take place supposedly in the interests of students. "We can imagine schools and individual learners using this 'digital ocean' to inform decisions about learning," explains one research report commissioned from the education giant Pearson (DiCerbo and Behrens 2014). This same data, however, can also be sold to marketers at a profit; or stolen from universities which haven't invested as much in Internet security as they should have (Watters 2014a). For edtech providers even to acknowledge that there is a tradeoff between learning and privacy here would be an improvement for many of them, but even that formulation assumes that big data is needed to get at the true nature of learning. What if it isn't?

After all, aren't professors supposed to be the ones who are experts on learning? Why do they need big data to tell them what learning is when some of us have been seeing it our classrooms for decades now? This is where the subject of assessment becomes important for us, even if it is not directly related to IT. Professors in the United States (and increasingly throughout the world) have been asked with increasing frequency in recent years to prove that students are actually learning the subjects that they're being taught. On one level, this is a difficult demand to resist. After all, university is expensive. Nobody wants all the money and time that students invest in themselves to go to waste.

Unfortunately, the drive to assess learning outcomes has the inevitable side effect of driving administrations to pressure professors to create the kind of assignments that can be quantified and therefore evaluated most simply. The people directly applying that pressure are instructional designers. This vocation has grown in recent years precisely because online education can be so easily monitored and assessed. As Lisa Lane, an historian with a great deal of experience teaching online describes this phenomenon:

> It's like making a movie. And I want to be Orson Welles – writer, director, actor. It's my class. I write it when I create the syllabus and collect the materials. I direct it when I teach and assist students. I act when I'm lecturing or presenting. But now that we've professionalized 'instructional design' (and other aspects of education that used to be considered support rather than primary functions), I feel there's a movement afoot to have me just act. Someone else has a degree that says they are more qualified than I am to design my class, in collaboration with me as the 'content expert.' They want to do the writing, create the storyboard, tell me what the 'best practices' are.
> *(Lane 2013)*

Instructional designers are not subject experts. They're supposedly learning experts. It is easy to imagine professors using them as a resource rather than seeing them as competitors, but this requires that everyone has a thorough understanding of their respective roles. "Best practices" are only best if everyone agrees on particular learning outcomes and this is by no means assured. It undoubtedly varies between disciplines and even varies within disciplines. The freedom to teach implies that different professors will have different goals.

Who controls the process of creating and carrying out online education will shape whether those online courses are worth the tuition fees that students pay to take them. "I have taught many online courses," explained one longtime adjunct faculty member in *Inside Higher Education*.

> We have tapped about 10 percent of the potential of online courses for teaching. But rather than exploring the untapped 90 percent, the college where I taught online wanted to standardize every course with a template designed by tech people with no input from instructors.

What's the matter with standardization?

> I want to design amazing online courses: courses so intriguing and intuitive and so easy to follow no one would ever need a tutorial. I want to design courses that got students eager to explore new things...Is anyone interested in this?
>
> *(Anonymous 2015)*

While this anonymous faculty member was obviously constrained by their contingent status, the lack of interest their administration has for this kind of course would presumably affect every professor at their university.

Who wins if online classes become nothing but dumbed-down versions of face-to-faces courses? The most obvious winners in this arrangement are cash-hungry administrators. Perhaps they share the preference of instructional designers for quantifiable results coming out of all classes regardless of discipline out of conviction, but the money from cookie-cutter online courses delivered by a reserve army of adjunct labor would be an enticing ulterior motive. Instructional designers aren't tenured. Many of them aren't even faculty. Once they've performed their task of reconfiguring any particular course or program, they can be let go in order to find other educations to design. The professors and the students who remain, however, have to live with the results.

Like instructional designers, the various private companies that provide education technologies to universities have little interest in the teaching philosophies and prerogatives of individual professors. They want to sell their product, and keep selling that product into the future. For that reason, they tend to target administrations rather than individual professors. In the case of learning management systems (an educational technology so important that we'll come back to it in a later chapter), this kind of focus is entirely understandable. For other technologies, any other reason besides increasing their business is unclear.

These kinds of deals are usually justified for the sake of maintaining learning excellence, but whether that is true depends upon one's definition of excellence. Adopting the language of assessment and instructional design, even using terms like "best practices," favors the kinds of results that can be measured on the kinds of standardized tests that these publishers will be happy to sell to you in order to prove their worth. Pearson even has its own research arm that will help faculty move towards the educational goals that their products promote and measure (Feldstein 2014, the second part of this sentence is our opinion, not Michael Feldstein's). What it doesn't promote is the subtle kind of deeper learning that an intense, well-taught face-to-face class can provide.

"I'm not opposed to disruption;" writes the historian Leslie Madsen-Brooks of Idaho State University,

> rather, I'm skeptical about the kind of disruption start-ups and tech folks promise: 'paradigm-shifting' technology that improves university teaching and learning. The truth is, many of these start-ups clearly have no idea what actually works in higher ed and know little about the direction university teaching

and learning have moved in the last 10 years, because they're trying to take us backward, not forward.

(Madsen-Brooks 2013)

While there are plenty of well-meaning people working in the edtech space who would disagree with this assessment, it is clear that many of them have a completely different conception of "what works" from professors like Madsen-Brooks.

Notice how Madsen-Brooks does not dismiss technology out of hand. Plenty of professors, teaching both online and off, have adopted at least some online tools that help them teach better. These include videos, blogging, digital publishing, interactive games, even Twitter, let alone aspects of learning management systems that their universities make available to them. What's most important for the sake of education is that they continue to have the freedom to access those tools that best suit the circumstances of their individual classes, whether they are sanctioned by their university or not.

Of course, a class that uses no technology at all is not necessarily a bad one. Lectures, so often derided by edtech enthusiasts, have their place in higher education when done well. Lecturing is an excellent way to convey a lot of information in a limited period of time, just as discussion is an excellent way to encourage critical thinking in students. A good class will include a mixture of both (mixed also with other approaches), the ratio being a function of where the course in question appears in the curriculum, among other considerations.

Learn online and you may never even know what your professor looks like. Take a class from a good lecturer and they'll entertain you, they'll react to your reactions and they'll offer to see you in office hours if you have any additional questions. You can even bring your assigned reading with you when you go. When you're done with the class, they may even fill out a letter of recommendation to help you get a job or get admitted to the graduate program of your choice. This would obviously be much harder for lecturers to do if they don't have the opportunities to get to know their students personally both inside the classroom and around a physical campus.

For those of us who care about education, teaching is a craft. We refine our lectures, write the best questions for discussions into our old copies of classic textbooks and do our best to get our students thinking. But now we're told that isn't good enough. In this new crisis atmosphere, professors are told that they have to adapt to a new way of educating because economic necessity requires such a thing. If your job depends upon a bottom line that can be measured easily rather than abstract thought processes that can't be measured at all, it becomes obvious which consideration will win out when these two things come into conflict.

That's why sitting back for as long as possible and teaching the way it's always been done shouldn't be an option. Eventually, the Internet is going to catch up, and when it does, the fact that any particular professor teaches better face-to-face than the vast majority of online instructors will not be much of a help because online classes will be totally normalized by then. The longer such classes are deemed acceptable, the harder it will become to resist them once disruption strikes every corner of university life.

Too many forces are pushing for acceptance of online education (if not its actual success at promoting learning) to reverse course. As the Internet analyst Clay Shirky has explained, "The digital revolution in higher education has already happened. No one noticed" (Shirky 2015). Recognizing this fact, it becomes imperative that every professor works to support the kinds of online education that do have merit and that do not destroy faculty's ability to exercise their expertise, since that is what makes education educational. As none other than Stanford's John Hennessy has explained, educational technology works "only with intense collaboration of faculty who touch the lives of our students every single day" (Jaschik 2015). While collaboration does not mean that faculty members are necessarily in the driver's seat with respect to all classroom decisions, it certainly means that they play an essential role in steering the ship.

Under such an arrangement, administrators should try persuasion first before mass firings, carrots ahead of sticks. We believe that technology can help professors in every discipline to teach better, as long as that technology remains under their control. Offering that control is a way to get them to employ educational technology willingly, which will ultimately magnify its effects in the classroom, as faculty could then pick the technologies that serve the educational needs of their students and reject the ones that don't.

Think of the money that would be saved on expensive licensing contracts for learning management systems with non-essential features added to make them seem more attractive without enhancing their main function, which most faculty members don't even use. Think of the improvements in efficiency that would occur if faculty members could focus on technologies that help them teach rather than those that can be used to track their every interaction with their students. Think of the exciting skills that students will learn.

Making this vision possible will require a broader definition of academic freedom than the one that so many educational technology enthusiasts are currently using. According to the American Association of University Professors,[1] "The freedom to teach includes the right of the faculty to select the materials, determine the approach to the subject, make the assignments, and assess student academic performance in teaching activities for which faculty members are individually responsible" (AAUP 2013b). While it is easy to see how edtech tools could affect all these things, such tools are not explicitly mentioned in that statement. If academic freedom does not include control over the technology one employs when teaching, professors could easily become the first prominent casualties of the disruption that so many educational technology advocates crave. Even if professors remain able to teach the content they want, they risk losing the ability to teach the kinds of skills that go with that content if those skills are not easily taught in an online setting.

More importantly, the spread of MOOCs——courses with content provided by professors whom students will never meet——could lead to the abandonment of skilled educational labor entirely, since there is no reason to pay people who went to graduate school to learn content if that content has already been purchased from an off-campus provider. If that nightmare scenario were to come about, professors might still have the freedom to teach whatever content they wanted, but they would be able to exercise it only while standing in the unemployment line, and students would be stuck with an impersonal, automated education. This particular kind of educational technology is the subject of the next chapter.

Note

1 We are both members of the AAUP. JR is co-President of the Colorado Caucus and a member of its National Council. JP is Vice-President of the Colorado State University—Pueblo chapter. For more on the AAUP, visit http://aaup.org.

3

MOOCs

The MOOC Revolution

"Welcome to the college education revolution," wrote Thomas Friedman on his op-ed platform for the *New York Times* in 2012 (Friedman 2012). Friedman was writing about Massive Open Online Courses (MOOCs). Friedman's newspaper famously called 2012 "the Year of the MOOC," and just the possibility that such a revolution might be happening was enough to inspire an attempt by the Board of Visitors of the University of Virginia to attempt to fire that school's president in that same year (Pappano 2012). While the hype surrounding MOOCs has ebbed since then, MOOCs remain a significant presence in higher education, both in terms of total number of students participating in them and as part of the discussion of its possible future. Therefore, understanding what they are and how they might affect faculty in the future remains imperative for everyone interested in promoting quality instruction.

The term MOOC was first employed by a group of academics in 2008 for a course on *Connectivism and Connective Knowledge* at Canada's Athabasca University. That course was co-taught by George Siemens (then of Athabasca) and Stephen Downes from the National Research Council of Canada. Their goal was for students to create distributed content across the Internet using tools like WordPress. The key to the course was the daily newsletter, which included links to recommended articles and other content around the web which students could then discuss, or not. Even though that initial MOOC wasn't for credit, it still attracted about 2200 students worldwide (Haber 2014), (Downes and Siemens 2008). No videos of superstar lecturers were involved.

This model has come to be known as a *cMOOC* (the "c" stands for connectivist) and it has become an inspiration for instructors in many disciplines to experiment with different pedagogical models in which students take charge of their own learning. A cMOOC might not even have a start or end date, and participants have little expectation of ever getting a course credit. Perhaps the best known of these MOOCs is DS106, a digital storytelling class that originated at the University of Mary Washington in Virginia and has been running continuously for years. cMOOCs require little infrastructure and their contents are generally distributed across a wide variety of sites.

Spreading knowledge for knowledge's sake is certainly a good thing. Connectivist courses, in other words cMOOCs that remain in the control of individual professors with the best of motives could be a real addition to the universe of higher education options, as long as they stay a supplement to existing options rather than as a replacement. Unfortunately, we do not live in an ideal world. There is a political economy of MOOCs that matters just as much as their technological structure, especially for those who will never teach in or learn from a MOOC over the course of their academic careers.

Another kind of MOOC has drawn the most attention in the press because it has a much higher potential to disrupt the way that higher education operates. In 2011, Sebastian Thrun (then of Stanford University) opened up his class on Artificial Intelligence to the world on the Internet and 160,000 students from 190 countries enrolled (Selingo 2014). Inspired more by the model of Khan Academy (a resource for secondary schools that originally appeared on YouTube) Thrun and his co-teacher Peter Norvig were the center of the course and starred in all the videos. Brief film segments were followed by multiple-choice quizzes in order for students to be able to demonstrate their knowledge. This model has come to be known as an *xMOOC*, and, of the two MOOC models available, it has many more students because it is designed to be gigantic—tens of thousands of students in many cases, rather than a few hundred.

Because of the success of his MOOC, Thrun left Stanford and went on to found Udacity, the first private MOOC company. Coursera and edX (a partnership between MIT and Harvard that isn't private but often acts as if it is) soon followed. Udacity has been most successful in offering job training for corporations, while Coursera and edX (which isn't strictly a company) earn most of their revenue selling certificates of completion to students who finish their courses.

These commercial xMOOC providers favor courses that are modeled on regular university courses like Thrun's original artificial intelligence class. In reference to the MOOCs produced by MIT with edX, Kevin Carey writes, "The university simply took the very good courses it was already offering and translated them, as accurately as possible, onto the edX platform" (Carey 2015). While MOOCs may appear to be the same courses offered at the prestigious universities, the act of moving those online changes them in many important ways. Most notably, the tuition-paying students who are physically present at those universities have much better access to their professors (or at least the support system at the university in which they are enrolled) than anybody just watching videos from home. Even the instructor for a 500-person lecture course at a gigantic state university has office hours and an email address. In MOOCs, noted an op-ed in the *New York Times* by a writer who took many of them at once, the instructors were only "slightly more accessible than the pope or Thomas Pynchon" (Jacobs 2013).

In an xMOOC, videotaped lectures by superstar professors at elite institutions are the main means of conveying information. Multiple-choice quizzes are the main means of student evaluation. While online fora invariably exist, where students can ask questions of the instructor and each other, only a small percentage of MOOC participants generally make use of them. As a result, MOOCs have been plagued by extremely high drop-out rates and a great deal of criticism on both educational and political grounds. According to a 2013 study by a graduate student at The Open University in the United Kingdom named Katy Jordan, less than 7 percent of students who sign up for these MOOCs ever complete them. That figure cuts across MOOCs from all disciplines (Parr 2013). These high attrition rates are one of the most obvious differences between MOOCs and other online courses.

In fact, the worst mistake anyone examining online education can make is to conflate MOOCs with other, smaller online courses. While all MOOCs take place online, not all online courses are MOOCs. A regular online course is usually small enough that someone can track the progress and offer guidance to every student enrolled in the course. Good online classes take pedagogical practice seriously. xMOOCs, as an inherent function of their very largeness, don't. That's why many professors who have been teaching small online courses in a thoughtful and deliberate manner deeply resent the attention that MOOCs have received. MOOCs distract from innovative online pedagogy that they've been practicing for sometimes as long as a decade or more.

The astronomically high student-to-faculty ratios in xMOOCs go a long way towards explaining their high drop-out rates. Nevertheless, this same feature explains the appeal of MOOCs to cash-strapped administrators of all kinds since fewer faculty and many more students would dramatically improve any university's bottom line. That's why MOOCs could (at least in theory) put faculty at non-elite universities on the unemployment line. If huge xMOOCs become both efficient and generally accepted, they could conceivably put entire universities out of business. Even cMOOCs, employed as a replacement for traditional courses, could theoretically lead to university campuses being replaced by giant online programs.

The (Many) Problems with MOOCs

How worried then, should today's faculty be? Should most of us be looking for our second careers now? We don't think so, but we do recommend that today's faculty pay close attention to developments in the MOOC space so that they can influence the future of higher education in a way that's good for them and their students at the same time. In *How the University Works*, Marc Bousquet writes about the "academic-capitalist fantasy of unlimited accumulation, dollars for credits nearly unmediated by faculty labor." He argues,

This is really a version of one of the oldest fantasies in industrial history, the fantasy of profit without workers. If only the investor could build an entirely mechanized factory! With the push of a button, cars and snowboards and washing machines would come out the other end.

(Bousquet and Nelson 2008, 58)

For faculty to survive in this new world of wired higher education, they will have to do more to justify their own existence. They have to dispel this particular kind of academic–capitalist fantasy.

To do that will require attacking the very possibility of an academic assembly line.

[W]ith a mechanized higher ed, a line of tuition payers could be run through automated courses that provide then with the 'necessary information,' and out the other end would emerge nurses! teachers! engineers! sports psychologists!

(Bousquet and Nelson 2008, 58)

Faculty members are at Point A, students are at countless Points B, and administrators sit at Point C, simply cashing the tuition checks. Coursera's MOOCs offer these administrators the opportunity to cut out Point A almost entirely. Yes, they might have to pay the glorified teaching assistants to tend to MOOC administration duties, but they could be easily replaced by anyone at the other end of an Internet connection. Universities certainly wouldn't be compelled to give these poor educators anything like a living wage or anything that even faintly resembles tenure.

The easiest part of any xMOOC to automate would be the lectures. Once taped and in the possession of university administrators they could at least in theory be cued up indefinitely. After all, since making a MOOC can cost as much as $250,000, it wouldn't be efficient to go back and record every lecture again each time a MOOC is given (Kolowich 2013c). Therefore, it becomes impossible for any MOOC to adapt to changing times or even just a changing audience. While this might possibly be considered acceptable for a MOOC on anatomy and physiology, which is mostly about memorizing facts, what about any subject which requires critical thinking?

As an example, this point is certainly important for history classes, since lay people tend to assume that as the past is past it therefore never changes. Anybody who knows what the word "historiography" means knows that this is not true at all. While Frederick Jackson Turner may have been the greatest historian of his era, putting a nineteenth-century historian like Frederick Jackson Turner in front of today's students would be a terrible disservice to everyone involved. Similarly, though much of the mathematics taught to university students is decades or hundreds of years old, it is not unchanging, nor can mathematical reasoning and problem solving be taught in the same manner as the memorization of rote facts.

Like letting MOOC lectures become frozen in amber, the practice of peer grading is another sacrifice to the difficulty in employing enough labor to offer quality teaching at such a huge scale. It's also a reason for the lack of rigor in classes that use it. The term peer grading describes the use of students to grade other students' written work in courses like English or history that generally depend upon written essays in order to evaluate student learning. No single professor (even with a team of teaching assistants) could ever hope to read, comment on, and evaluate the work of thousands of students, so MOOCs in these subject areas generally require students to do this work instead.

Unfortunately, it takes a rare kind of student who knows enough to evaluate the work of their colleagues when they are just learning the same material themselves. Assuming they somehow know as much about what constitutes good writing as their professor does, they are unlikely to exercise the same care when evaluating their peers because they are seldom incentivized by the peer grading system to do so.[1] The general practice is to offer students doing that grading a detailed rubric to use as a guide. There have been a variety of ingenious workarounds to solve this dilemma (see, for example, Wiggins (2014)). Nonetheless, the fact that any workaround is necessary demonstrates the kind of thinking that made MOOCs popular in the first place—solve the economic problems associated with higher education first, and worry about the quality of that education second.

Automated essay grading is an even bigger problem than peer grading in this regard. In recent years, computer essay grading has become more sophisticated and it has been championed by MOOC providers because of its obvious benefits for their bottom lines. EdX, for instance, has been conducting and sharing pioneering research in this field. Georgia Tech has plans to do something similar within its all-MOOC computer science MA program with Udacity (Haynie 2014). Some studies have suggested that the computers can grade just as well as regular human graders do, but every teacher knows that it's not the grades that matter when learning how to write—it's the comments (Kolowich 2014). It takes much, much more time to write comments on essays for precisely this reason than it does to read them. Even "A" students learn from the reasons their instructor puts at the bottom of their essay as to why their essay got an "A". That's how they know what to do again next time. Anyone with any grade lower than that needs the instructor's comments to know what to do better.

Then there's the issue of fostering creativity when the grading criteria are chosen so that they can be evaluated by computers. Machines can teach you rules, but they can never teach you how to break them, or especially when breaking the rules is the appropriate response to a particular situation. No wonder Sebastian Thrun wants to do corporate training now. The people most willing to pay for his services are perhaps the only people in society who want education to produce "yes men" who will never check back. You may call that what you want, but it certainly isn't a profound educational experience. No matter how powerful future computers eventually become, only other well-trained human beings[2] can teach students when and how to break rules.

Despite such problems, plenty of universities that have gotten on the MOOC bandwagon argue that improving instruction on campus is the main reason that they began these kinds of experiments. As a report from Harvard's Provost Office explains,

HarvardX builds on the premise that online education complements, rather than competes with, the teaching we do in our classrooms and labs. From the outset, HarvardX was intended to advance learning both on and off campus and to set a standard for excellence in the production of online courses.

(Garber 2015)

That whole report, like so much written about online learning since the year of the MOOC, conflates MOOCs with online learning in general. Anyone who has actually taught for a living understands that there is a difference between teaching a class of ten and a class of ten thousand. Rather than help, the most logical way to integrate tools from MOOCs into substantially smaller classes is to discover what parts of those smaller classes can be automated.

Ordinary university students simply can't teach themselves alone. While Harvard professors may be excellent scholars and teachers, they are not so much better than everyone else that merely their taped presence can improve upon the teaching of a living, breathing human stationed in the same classroom as the student all semester. As even online education advocate Stanford's John Hennessy recognizes, cheapness "When I think about MOOCs, the advantage –the ability to prepare a course and offer it without personal interaction – is what makes them inexpensive and makes them very limited" (Jaschik 2015). While this might make sense for a MOOC provider's bottom line, it is not a good recipe for quality higher education.

Of course, the quality of education has many dimensions that go beyond the nature of the interaction between the teacher and the student. There's the issue of rigor, for example. To make up for the fact that MOOC students do not pay tuition fees, the universities that produce MOOCs along with their partner companies have tried to attract and keep as many students as possible—often tens of thousands of students at a time, since a large number of students give MOOC providers the data that they might be able to monetize someday. This creates a host of MOOC-specific problems around the inherent tension between the financial interests of these private entities and any interest that a professor might have in maintaining rigor in their classes.

Many MOOCs from Coursera have no required textbook, probably because too much reading might scare off potential participants who could eventually become a source of revenue for that company, whether they finish the course or not. When the *Chronicle of Higher Education* surveyed 103 professors who taught MOOCs, the publication asked if they thought that the students who passed those courses deserved course credit at the elite institutions where the MOOC originated. Seventy-two percent of them said no, presumably because they don't meet the work standards for what students do in the face-to-face versions of the same classes (Kolowich 2013a).

Another problem with MOOCs that stems directly from the fact that they are online is the difficulty that any instructor would have in trying to tell if their students are cheating. While it's hard enough to catch cheating in an online setting, creating a security state for tens of thousands of students at once is simply just not possible. Rather than create a secure environment for everyone, MOOC providers charge students for a "certified" degree, which requires them to submit to the same kind of security regimen found in regular universities' online courses. As was the case with regular online courses, this problem hardly exists in the bricks-and-mortar education, since preventing cheating is usually a natural result of an instructor's physical presence in the same room as their students.

MOOCs, on the other hand, have to function on a pedagogical model that leaves students to fend through the educational process almost entirely on their own—otherwise they wouldn't be MOOCs. Certainly, well-prepared, self-disciplined students can benefit greatly from having access to information presented in an impersonal MOOC format. This may explain why so many students who succeed in MOOCs already have some sort of degree—eight out of ten enrolled in MOOCs given by the University of Michigan and the University of Pennsylvania (Selingo 2013). But out of the entire population of possible university students, how many of them are well-prepared and self-disciplined? To limit future educational opportunities to this particular model minority would be to turn the purpose of education on its head.

Unfortunately, much of the money to fund MOOCs will come from budgets that might have been used for face-to-face teaching. More importantly, much of the money that MOOCs might potentially make at some time in the future will be at the expense of already cash-strapped universities, probably from funds that currently pay most of our salaries. Even Sebastian Thrun admits, "The belief that education can be replaced by a computer program is a myth, driven in part by media eager to play upon people's fears in an otherwise important, constructive debate" (Shen 2013). Unfortunately, that fact won't stop some cash-strapped administrators from trying to do so anyway.

Even if xMOOCs fail to survive in their current, mostly-automated form, they still have the potential to do irreparable harm to the demand for the kind of labor that well-trained faculty can provide. Mitchell Duneier, a Princeton sociology professor who once taught a MOOC for Coursera, noted this possibility when he stopped teaching it in 2013. He did so because Coursera asked him about licensing parts of his MOOC to other schools so that they could use his course content in a blended classroom format. "I've said no, because I think that it's an excuse for state legislatures to cut funding to state universities," Duneier told the *Chronicle of Higher Education* (Parry 2013). Those cost savings would presumably come by replacing well-paid tenured or tenure-track sociologists with lesser-paid adjuncts. Indeed, if a school licensed enough of Duneier's MOOC, there would be no reason to hire a sociologist at all. They could be replaced with a person trained simply to run the platform upon which the MOOC resides.

Thanks to the ability of anyone with an Internet connection to access any MOOC, the recognition of MOOCs for official course credit is ultimately self-defeating for universities that are not prestigious enough to create their own. "If students at some point have the option of substituting a free or low-cost MOOC taught by a celebrity professor at an elite institution," writes the Silicon Valley entrepreneur Martin Ford, "that alone could be a major financial blow to the financial stability of many lower-ranked schools" (Ford 2015, 143). Thankfully, this future hasn't happened yet, but that's not for want of trying.

Arizona State University (in partnership with edX), has created the option of an all-MOOC freshman year (Agarwal 2015). So far, the response to this program has been less than earth-shaking. Out of the 34,086 registrants in ASU's first set of classes, only 323 of them earned the right to request credit for completing a course. Even then, there is no guarantee that all of those 323 will pay Arizona State the fee required to earn credit (Straumsheim 2015a). Matt Reed, writing on his blog at *Inside Higher Education*, offers his theory why these numbers are so low.

> [T]o the extent that the partnership was supposed to be about opening pathways to bachelor's degrees, it doesn't come close to comparing to the already-established route of starting at a community college – in this case, I used the tuition rate of Maricopa Community College, the largest feeder to ASU – and transferring".
>
> *(Reed 2015)*

Maybe the old ways are old for a reason.

Technically, when MOOCs are adapted to a traditional university setting they are no longer MOOCs because they are no longer open. Students have to pay tuition fees in order to enroll in them. Years into the MOOC boom and there have been countless problems with students paying for them in order to gain real credit. For example, Colorado State University – Global (our university system's entirely online campus) formed a partnership with Udacity to allow students to gain credit by successfully completing their computer science MOOC. Successful completers would only have to pay an $89 processing fee. That offer had zero takers (Haber 2014, 106). One of the reasons that Arizona State's all-MOOC freshman year has failed to take off may be that all those credits can only be used to graduate through Arizona State. Elsewhere—including the job market—MOOC credits get very little respect. Perhaps there's a good reason for that.

While community colleges (at least for now) can compete with an all-MOOC education in terms of price, this is not their only advantage. All conventional classrooms have advantages over MOOCs on pedagogical terms. Try to see things from the students' perspective rather than the perspective of someone who is concerned only with the finances of an organization and not the larger concerns, and the superiority of face-to-face instruction should be obvious. Living, breathing professors can answer questions. They can provide motivation. They can see their students' faces and adjust their lessons accordingly. MOOCs, on the other hand, have many of the disadvantages of the largest lecture classes in huge auditoriums at huge universities without providing the teaching assistants and writing centers that make those kinds of classes at least moderately bearable.

Most professors, who did nothing during a job interview but lecture in fifteen minute chunks, following up on each chunk with a single multiple-choice question, would never be hired at any university that we've ever encountered. Good teaching always involves a give and take between the instructor and the student. When the students don't understand what the instructor means, as an experienced instructor can tell even without a spoken question, the instructor explains it to them a different way. It makes no sense simply to repeat the same words over and over again.

What the MOOC does have is reach, but that's the product of the medium by which it's delivered, not the quality of education that MOOCs provide. Indeed, very popular instructors with large audiences across the Internet, sometimes known as "superprofessors" in the literature and commentary about MOOCs, are often giddy with the newfound attention. "You can take the blue pill and go back to your classroom and lecture to your 20 students," said Sebastian Thrun when he left Stanford for Udacity, "but I've taken the red pill and I've seen Wonderland" (Hsu 2012).

This kind of attitude has led to serious abuses by a few superprofessors. A review of a 2013 Coursera MOOC on songwriting out of the prestigious Berklee College of Music, declares, "Quite simply, this course is an advert." Apparently, as it became clear that the instructor could not cover everything about this subject in the time he allotted, he peddled his own books and DVDs to his captive audience worldwide (Tracey 2013). Do that in your face-to-face classes and most administrations will accuse you of a conflict of interest, but since there is as yet no precedent for what goes in a MOOC, many kinds of ethical line-crossing become possible. One superstar MIT physicist, for example, has been accused of sexually harassing multiple students online (Straumsheim 2015b).

Even those MOOC professors who want to make their MOOCs as similar to their regular courses as possible face terrible restrictions upon their traditional prerogatives. Karen Head of Georgia Tech, who taught a composition MOOC (once) on the Coursera platform, described in the *Chronicle of Higher Education* how working with a private company limited her traditional prerogatives as a teacher. "My limited ability to make key pedagogical choices is the most frustrating aspect of teaching a MOOC," she wrote. "Because of the way the Coursera platform is constructed, such wide-ranging decisions have been hard-coded into the software – decisions that seem to have no educational rationale and that thwart the intent of our course" (Head 2013a). Head had a team of nineteen people designing her course with her (Head 2013b).

In this manner, people other than the professor whose name is on the course end up having a disproportionate impact on how MOOC faculty operates their classes—certainly much more than they might in ordinary face-to-face classes. This kind of intervention would simply not be economical or feasible if the instruction wasn't occurring online in front of tens of thousands of students. In ordinary face-to-face classes, an instructor can safely dismiss the advice of instructional designers and other consultants. When tens of thousands of dollars are needed just to get your course off the ground, faculty members have to give up some control almost by definition.

Sometimes these limitations on professorial prerogatives have become explicit. Consider the experience of Paul-Olivier Dehaye. A mathematician at the University of Zurich, Dehaye was teaching a MOOC about how to understand MOOCs. When Dehaye asked Coursera for all the data associated with his MOOC so that he could discuss their policies as part of his class, the company locked him out of his own course. Dehaye is now suing Coursera as a result (Boie and Grassegger 2015). In other words, while star professors are the public face of MOOCs, the people really holding the power are the private companies that provide the platform. To them, higher education is nothing but a series of isolated, standardized content factories. That philosophy may eventually yield an extraordinary return for Coursera's investors, but the savings that generate that return will most likely come from labor cost savings.

Think of the kind of arrangement that Mitchell Duneier rejected for his sociology MOOC. Smaller universities could pay to license content provided by superprofessors working for big MOOC providers. Administrators who paid for that content would then pressure faculty to use it. The university, in turn, would then no longer have to pay for faculty on campus who know that content. In this manner, tenure track or even tenured faculty members could be replaced by adjuncts or glorified teaching assistants, whose only job is to make sure the MOOC software is functioning and to run multiple-choice tests through the grading machine.

A situation like this has already happened at San Jose State University in California. In 2013, professors in the Philosophy Department there refused to use an edX MOOC created by the Harvard philosopher Michael Sandel because they did not want to help "replace professors, dismantle departments, and provide a diminished education for students in public universities" (Kolowich 2013b). The administration there did not force the philosophers to use the MOOC. Instead, they moved it to the English Department where they could use less-qualified English teaching assistants to run the course (San Jose State University Philosophy Department 2013). In short, as long as administrations are in control of technology, they can always use it as a weapon against faculty and educational quality if they so choose.

The MOOCS of the Future

Even as the number of MOOCs keeps growing, the hype that once surrounded them has started to ebb. The most obvious turning point in the history of MOOC hype was November 2013, when Sebastian Thrun expressed his misgivings about them in an interview with the magazine *Fast Company*. "We were on the front pages of newspapers and magazines," he told reporter Max Chafkin, "and at the same time, I was realizing, we don't educate people as others wished, or as I wished. We have a lousy product" (Chafkin 2013). Because of these concerns, Udacity switched its emphasis to creating professional development opportunities for companies that need their employees retrained rather than competing with the world's great universities.

The key difference between paying students and the core constituency of Udacity or Coursera is that the people taking MOOCs have not incurred a monetary risk. Therefore, there is no penalty for them to drop in or drop out as they please. Move a MOOC inside a bricks-and-mortar university and students have motivation since they're paying for the course. Unfortunately, the quality of the education doesn't get any better. Charge for MOOCs and the free riders go away, but something worse happens—those who are left are paying for an inferior product. Administrators might have lower labor costs, but students suffer.

People who are thrilled with the possibility of taking MOOCs are generally people who have nothing better to do and are comparing MOOCs to no education at all. University-age or university-ready people will be comparing it to their previous forms of instruction. Even if they get their secondary school degree online, they will at least have experience with a living, breathing instructor on the other end of the computer screen. They will not pay thousands of dollars to be treated like an app. Besides, even if they are willing to pay, there's no guarantee that banks will keep on loaning to students whatever they need to pay for an all-MOOC university education.

On the other hand, perhaps MOOCs can drive down the cost of university by making it possible for self-motivated students to learn without having to pay for all the amenities like new campus buildings, football teams, and climbing walls in the gym. If so, students who can't afford university will then skip conventional campuses for an all-MOOC education, since at least some students really only care about getting a degree.[3] Existing universities will have to cut prices as a result. Some schools will not survive.

Another possibility runs something like this: students love fraternity parties and football games and contact with their professors. Therefore, they will refuse to accept an all-MOOC education at any price; neither will employers, who will quickly see that MOOCs do a substantially worse job at teaching university students the skills needed for the jobs of the future than a face-to-face class does. Perhaps there will be a place for MOOCs in the higher education ecosystem of the future to train people who have already graduated or to entertain smart people with a lot of time on their hands, but they will never lead to anything like a revolution.

A more likely possibility is a bifurcated situation where those who can afford university attend conventional universities, while those who can't make do with MOOCs. Another is a MOOC industry that caters to vocational education and professional development, like Udacity is trying to do since Sebastian Thrun's now infamous pivot cited above. A third possibility is MOOCs remaining a popular (and possibly even profitable) tool for a vast number of lifelong learners, rather than an instrument that could displace the university experience as we have always known it. No matter what, suggests Martin Weller of the UK's Open University, "MOOCs will need to be targeted to meet very specific aims and audiences" (Weller 2015).

Unlike a lot of other critics of this particular educational technology, we have both taken (different) MOOCs and completed them. While we remain critical of many of the pedagogical sacrifices made in those classes, we enjoyed the experience. We don't want to take anyone's MOOC away, but the idea of leaving any student no other option but MOOCs should leave every professor cold. Ultimately, though, it's not the MOOCs that are the problems. They would be an asset to the world—nerdy edu-tainment for the intellectual crowd—if it weren't for the entrepreneurs, venture capitalists and administrators who are assisting MOOC providers by supplanting living, breathing professors with their videos and computer programs. What professors should fear then is not the MOOCs themselves, but the kind of university governance that makes this kind of abuse possible.

They should also worry about the kinds of technologies that enable MOOCs falling into the hands of people who don't have the best interests of students or faculty at heart. Even if MOOCs do not displace faculty entirely, we may still have to worry about them. In early 2015, Coursera began to switch its business strategy so that universities could use pieces of their MOOCs in place of conventional lectures. This change required the MOOC provider to rebuild its entire platform so that students and professors could access content "on demand" (Dodd 2015a).

The purpose of this is to facilitate the practice of flipping the classroom, which is covered in a later chapter in this book. However, for now it is worth noting that Coursera contracts with entire campuses rather than individual professors. Therefore faculty, particularly non-tenured faculty, could be under tremendous pressure to use Coursera's taped lectures to provide educational content, should their administrations contract for access to it.

The existence of MOOCs marketed directly at universities poses the question of whether faculty will run the educational technology of the future or whether the technology will run them. That's why every professor, online or in-person, needs to make it abundantly clear to their employer, their students, and the general public what they bring to the table when they're doing their job. That list should include knowledge, experience, insight and inspiration—among other traits. Faculty can win this debate as long as they can explain how their industry can still use technology to benefit students without becoming automated.

No matter what the exact future for MOOCs in higher education around the world is, the future of university instruction is too important to let its fate be left to chance. Society has an interest in educating students from all walks of life so that they can become the doctors, lawyers, and police officers of tomorrow. If that education becomes automated, its quality will suffer greatly. Therefore, even though the cost of a university education (at least in the United States) is way too high, limiting the prerogatives that professors can exercise in order to protect course quality amounts to destroying something valuable because it is not widely enough available.

Ultimately, if MOOCs can't serve as a real substitute for bricks-and-mortar higher education, what problem do they actually solve? They don't improve access to university because you can't get an all-MOOC degree. Indeed, it's hard enough at the present time to get university credit for a single class delivered as a MOOC. If you want more students to get a university education, then fund public universities better. If you want students to do better in class, then lower class sizes.

MOOCs are expensive to produce, and they don't generate any revenue (at least as long as they're given away for free). Even if MOOCs are used as labor-saving devices, the cost of labor is not what's driving up university costs. The existence of adjuncts is all the proof needed for that point since as their use has grown the price of academic labor has dropped precipitously. If you want to introduce more technology into classrooms, then create technologies that individual professors can use rather than technologies that can be employed by penny-pinching administrations in order to replace them.

Notes

1 It's important to differentiate peer grading from peer review, the practice of letting students read each other's papers. Certainly, some students can have a great deal to offer in the way of assistance to their peers. However, even the best students generally don't know enough actually to grade those papers and provide the kinds of commentary that will help those students do better next time. We believe that is the job of the professor.

2 Or, if they become possible, Turing-certified artificial intelligences. See the discussion in Chapter 6.

3 It's funny that despite MOOCs being free at the moment, just about everyone involved in this industry assumes that this will not last. Currently, companies like Coursera make their money from charging successful students for certificates that demonstrate that they completed the course. They are actively looking for new revenue streams. Eventually, that will be likely to include tuition, albeit a much cheaper tuition than established universities currently charge.

4

FREE/LIBRE/OPEN-SOURCE EDTECH

This chapter covers one of the most significant movements in IT for higher education—*free/libre/open-source software*—from the perspective of copyright law. This does require some legal technicalities, but we begin with a very concrete example of a license in a purely academic context.

Classroom EULAs

There are two general approaches to respond to the enormous economic pressures under which universities, particularly state universities in the United States, find themselves: decrease costs or increase revenues. There are many examples of the cost-cutting strategy, often by cutting or switching to cheaper instructors—a route to a largely (or entirely) adjunct faculty. Raising additional revenue nearly always involves increasing tuition, although some fun games are also played with course or program fees, or requirements that students live in expensive dorms, and so on.

Another potential revenue stream is the intellectual property created by faculty in the fertile environment of a university. For research universities, patents should be a great source of income, and while that is sometimes true, it turns out not to be entirely simple (see Ledford 2013). All universities do some teaching, however, so all could try to get more income than merely tuition fees from pedagogical intellectual property. The situation with textbooks and other instructional materials can be surprisingly disadvantageous to the universities as a whole, but materials produced in unbundling (see Chapter 5) can be monetized more easily (or so administrations seem to believe).

Mathematics is a largely service department at many smaller universities. It is mostly taught in service to other science and engineering fields or as general education courses designed to satisfy some sort of quantitative reasoning requirement. These service courses can be made to generate long-term income from the students, as follows. The end user license agreement (EULA) that all math students sign in each class now has the additional provision, skipping the first seventeen pages that one usually scrolls right past (the students generally don't read any part of the EULA), as follows—this one taken from a Calculus II course on our campus:

> The licensee *[these are the students, in the legalese of an EULA]* may use the techniques taught in this class, including, but not limited to, Integration by Parts, Trigonometric Substitution, Partial Fractions, Taylor Series Expansions, etc., including all of the techniques mentioned by name in the attached syllabus, with the exception of *U*-substitution (which is considered a basic human right by the World Intellectual Property Organization and so is not restricted in any way by this license) – hereafter to be called *the techniques* – so long as they remain enrolled as a full- or part-time student at an accredited institution of undergraduate education. Immediately upon disenrollment, by graduation or any other form of official termination of their student status, licensee shall cease and desist from using *the techniques* in any context whatsoever.
>
> For additional annual fee of $500, graduating licensees may purchase a *graduate's Calculus II license*, which permits up to 17 [seventeen] uses of *the techniques* per annum; other licenses allowing greater numbers of applications of *the techniques* (with attractive rates!) are available for graduates who are working in technical fields – please contact the University's *Intellectual Property Office*.
>
> There is also special *grad student license*, for only $250 per annum, which allows unlimited uses of *the techniques* while licensee is enrolled in an accredited Masters or Ph.D. program – which fee is *waived entirely* if that program is at one of the campuses of our university system.
>
> Finally, the licensee shall not, under any circumstance whatsoever, explain, demonstrate, or give helpful feedback or criticism on, *the techniques*, by any means oral, visual, mechanical, or electronic, in any context, applied or abstract, to any individual who is not the instructor of record or a registered student in this section of Calculus II.

The provost on our campus was particularly delighted with the clause of this EULA that waives license fees for our own graduate students, as it clearly helps to provide an economic incentive for students to consider our institution's Masters and Ph.D. programs—and boosting enrollment is always a good thing!

It is not difficult to enforce this EULA because students are generally quite aware of the value of *the techniques* they learn in a class like Calculus II, so they have little hesitation to pay real money for real value. (There are interestingly different enforcement issues for EULAs in College Algebra or Statistics, both courses taken by more of a mass audience: it is similar to the difference between the audience for a global pop star and one for some particular niche musical style.) They also understand that content providers will have no incentive to do what they do without the possibility to make a reasonable profit thereby—this is the basic rationale behind all of copyright law (and all of capitalism), which is in the very air that digital natives breathe.

Occasionally, there will be a student who not only violates the terms of this EULA, but in fact sets him or herself up as a direct competitor to the original course, maybe by teaching *the techniques* to a younger sibling or friend who has not taken the course officially and therefore not paid any of the specific tuition fees for that material. The very worst—whom we have dubbed *calculus pirates*—post detailed explanations of *the techniques* on public *math-sharing* websites, where they can be used by anyone (even terrorists and child pornographers). Such cases threaten our social and economic order so thoroughly that we must make public examples of these calculus pirates. Fortunately, there are many talented and experienced lawyers in this space, since it is exactly the kind of content distribution and protection so widely used in those countries which participate in the current international copyright regime.

Copyright I: Liberal Beginnings

Clearly that last bit was a joke. We do not yet attempt to enforce copyright law in the minds of our students, and students do not sign an EULA before starting all math classes (although some professors have students sign a *contract,* misusing the term, to commit as formally as possible to upholding expectations about their efforts). But this isn't really all that far-fetched when you consider how corporations have pushed copyright law over the last few decades.

In the United States, intellectual property law stems from Article I, Section 8, Clause 8, of the U.S. Constitution, known as the *Copyright Clause*, which reads:

> The Congress shall have Power To promote the Progress of Science and useful Arts, by securing for limited Times to Authors and Inventors the exclusive Right to their respective Writings and Discoveries.

This clause includes its own self-justification: the patent and copyright laws Congress creates, based on this constitutional authority, are intended to promote science and (useful?) arts. The idea was that a kind of monopoly power with limited duration over ideas, in patents, and writings, in copyright, would get those lazy bohemians off the couch to invent and to write, in the knowledge that they would be able to profit from their inventions and writings.

The implied argument here seems fairly simple:

(1) A greater production of, and new forms of, Science and useful Arts are a common good worthy of support.
(2) Inventors and artists must be offered the promise of future profits in order for them to be motivated to create more, and new, Science and useful Arts.
(3) An appropriate way to create a reasonable profit motive is to offer creators a monopoly of limited duration for their inventions and artistic creations.

Hopefully, no one will argue with (1), although *who* will support this common good and *how* are clearly questions that need to be addressed. One response, by the way, which attracts a level of enthusiasm that varies with changing political climate, is for the government to provide the support directly, perhaps by some kind of *National Science Foundation (NSF)* and *National Endowment for the Humanities (NEH)*, or similarly named agencies.

Point (2) approaches this good with the worldview of *liberalism*—not particularly surprising given that the Constitution was written in a moment when liberal politics were ascendant, and by political liberals.[1] Liberalism sees a way to produce the common good of Science and useful Arts by using a market funded by the consumers in which the creators will be motivated by the hope of profit to get up and do the creation.

One interesting thing about the classical period of liberalism, particularly when contrasted with the more extreme form of neoliberalism currently dominant in the United States (and elsewhere in the Global North), is that the Founders felt that neither completely pure free markets, nor too heavy government intervention were the best course. Pure free markets have so much uncertainty for potential innovators that they would hesitate to bring to market new Science and useful Arts in the fear that others would steal their ideas and then their profits. Too much government intervention could be swayed to the advantage of particular elites.

Instead, in point (3), they corrected the market by creating government-granted monopolies—patents and copyrights—while, at the same time, limiting their duration in order to avoid onerous, permanent economic fiefs. This mechanism is focused on boosting the *first-mover advantage* (Lieberman & Montgomery 1988) by reducing uncertainty, in certain market situations, about how an innovator will be able to profit after taking the risk of innovating.

Copyright II: The Mickey Mouse Era

Unfortunately, there are three obvious problems with the foundations of copyright law as described above, mostly related to points (2) and (3), and in the fundamental market-based approach. First of all, it is really an empirical question as to whether the best way to motivate creators is via the hope for future profits coming from limited-term monopoly control over their creations. Fortunately, some empirical research has been done, recently by Jessica Silbey, described in her book *The Eureka Myth* (Silbey 2014). Interviewing artists, scientists, and engineers, Silbey found that they did not talk about the limited monopolies awaiting their creations, but instead spoke largely about two issues: one along the lines of needing *a room of one's own* (with time, space, and autonomy) and the other having to do with cultivating social relationships, with their audiences, collaborators, and the eyes of posterity. Apparently the typical scientist or artist does not actually think much like a *homo œconomicus*.

Second, even assuming that creators are inspired by the idea of their future limited monopoly, it is not clear whether that monopoly is actually the way profit-maximizing creators would maximize their profits. For example, the author and activist Cory Doctorow has written about how giving away his books for free on his website at the same time they are sold in bookstores and on the Internet has helped him to make even more money (Doctorow 2008). Doctorow's anecdotal experience is also supported by a study (admittedly small) (Hilton III and Wiley 2010), which also found free e-books leading to increased sales of print books.[2] Both Doctorow and independently Amanda Palmer, in (Palmer 2014), emphasize the role of an artist's relationship with their audiences to explain their non-traditional (non-market- and -copyright-based) approaches.

Third, it makes sense to be careful about whether the limited monopoly approach is a market correction of the right size. We have just seen that some successful current artists feel (and act as if) these monopolies are unnecessary (or detrimental when exercised) even if very short, but there are reasons to think carefully about the long end of their duration as well. So, disregarding Silbey, Doctorow, and Palmer, and falling back on the pure monopoly-reward motivation, note that it is purported to be effective because of the risk-reduction by guaranteed future profit that it offers. But first-movers already have some significant advantages (although that can vary with the industry and product; see Lieberman and Montgomery (1988) for the surprisingly subtle story) so we do not want to give them so much additional power here that they establish de facto permanent monopoly control over their industries simply by virtue of having been the first to create a product there.

This last point is where the history of copyright in the last several decades seems to go completely off its (liberal) rails. Record labels and movie studios both made huge profits in the mid- and late-twentieth century in the United States and sought to protect the intellectual property that was the basis of their cash cows[3] —using copyright law. Essentially, very successful first-movers wanted to make their limited monopolies much longer, and to protect them against new technological threats in the Internet Age, by pushing a pair of Acts known as the *Sonny Bono Copyright Term Extension Act (CTEA)* and the *Digital Millennium Copyright Act (DMCA)*, both in 1998.

Prior to these two Acts, the specifics of copyrights, including what was covered and how, as well as the duration of a copyright, had been defined and then modified in a series of *Copyright Acts* dating 1790, 1909, and 1976. The term of copyrights started out as 14 years, plus 14 more years if renewed, and by 1976 became the life of the author plus 50 years, or simply 75 years in the case where there was no identifiable author, that is, anonymous works, works produced under a pseudonym, and works created for a corporation or other collective entity.

Then in 1998, with the CTEA, the term of copyrights was extended to the life of the author plus 70 years and, for works of corporate authorship, to the date of creation plus 120 years or date of publication plus 95 years, whichever comes first. Furthermore, these new lengths of copyrights applied *also to works already extant and already under copyright:* older works got a boost of profit-making lifetimes.

There is just no way this extension of the lifetimes of copyrights on existing works fits the original justification in the Copyright Clause of the Constitution. Increasing the prospects for future profits cannot be an incentive for the creation of *already existing works*, they exist already and no amount of additional incentive today will create more works in the past. That's just the way time works. Instead, one is left with the impression that the CTEA existed solely to continue the income being derived from already existing works by already wealthy and powerful corporations who had been first-movers quite some time before.

In particular, one consequence of the CTEA was to extend the life of the Walt Disney Company's copyright on the character *Mickey Mouse*, which would have otherwise run out at the end of 2003: under the CTEA, Mickey will remain a Disney employee until 1 January 2024. As it was found that Disney gave contributions to several of the politicians in Congress involved in passing the CTEA, (Ota 1998), it starts to seem that Disney (although certainly with the help of the Recording Industry Association of American (RIAA) and the Motion Picture Association of America (MPAA)) in some sense bought the copyright law it wanted. Some copyright activists have called the CTEA the *Mickey Mouse Protection Act* for this reason.

The other copyright law of 1998, the DMCA, is not so much a violation of the fundamental logic of the Copyright Clause as it is a hubristic overreach of powers which might, in some modest form, be necessary to protect basic copyright in the Internet Age. The reason is that to the extent that one believes in copyright which is anything like the original liberal version, the advent of the Internet as the primary distribution mechanism of most copyrighted materials presents an enormous technological problem.

This problem is somewhat masked by common parlance in the Internet Age which draws a distinction between *streaming* and *downloading* digital data. In fact, this distinction is a bit of science fiction, as there is absolutely no difference, in terms of bits[4] moving around on networks. What is different is that the software on the consumer end of a so-called streaming connection politely agrees to erase all of the bits the moment they are off the screen or out of the earbuds of the consumer.

As a consequence, digital data—music and movies, for example—in reality are distributed from vendors to consumers in a form which is very easy to steal, to copy and share in ways that violate the rights of the copyright holder. Of course, the same thing is true of any book, but with a physical book, before the advent of the Internet, it was a somewhat tedious process to copy and distribute infringing versions of the copyright-protected material. Not so for digital files. (To err is human; to screw things up hundreds of thousands of times a second requires a computer.)

One response of the middlemen was to create complex technological systems in an attempt to protect the digital data and to prevent them from being copied. These systems are called Digital Restrictions Management (DRM)[5] and none of them are actually secure against a determined adversary. This is because the data must actually be present and unwrapped from any DRM at some point, at the very least before going to the screen and earbuds on the consumer's machine. Therefore if the middleman follows a common DRM strategy of scrambling—formally *encrypting*—the data as they are in transit over the network, there must nevertheless be an unscrambling—*decrypting*—program on the consumer's device, which means a wily (and criminal) programmer can tinker with this program, or other programs on that device, to steal these decrypted data.

Fearing (with some reason) the high-speed copying and illegal distribution of copyrighted materials on the Internet, the RIAA and the MPAA (and others of their ilk) pushed for legislation to make it illegal to circumvent DRM on copyrighted digital data, and got the DMCA. Section 1201 of this Act states "No person shall circumvent a technological measure that effectively controls access to a work protected under this title," where "this title" refers to U.S. Code, Title 17, the entire law on copyright. Further,

> No person shall manufacture, import, offer to the public, provide, or otherwise traffic in any technology, product, service, device, component, or part thereof, that –
>
> (A) is primarily designed or produced for the purpose of circumventing a technological measure that effectively controls access to a work protected under this title;
> (B) has only limited commercially significant purpose or use other than to circumvent a technological measure that effectively controls access to a work protected under this title; or
> (C) is marketed [...] for use in a technological measure that effectively controls access to a work protected under this title....

Later it is also helpfully specified that in this subsection, "to 'circumvent a technological measure' means to descramble a scrambled work, to decrypt an encrypted work, or otherwise to avoid, bypass, remove, deactivate, or impair a technological measure...".

The courts have interpreted these anti-circumvention provisions very broadly, as have corporations and entities like the RIAA whose threats of litigation can be very intimidating, even if potential defendants hope they will prevail in the end. The phrase *offer to the public, provide, or otherwise traffic in* circumvention methods and devices, covers, it is alleged, even public academic discussion of security issues in DRM technologies and methods, even of some much more general aspects of computer security research. Some examples (from the very many possible) of how this has played out in the real world are:

- Russian programmer Dmitry Sklyarov, in the United States to give a conference presentation about security issues with e-book software from Adobe Systems, Inc., was arrested and prosecuted for violation of the DMCA §1201; see *US v. ElcomSoft and Sklyarov FAQ* (EFF 2011b).
- Threats of prosecution from the RIAA and an organization called the Secure Digital Music Initiative (SDMI) against Princeton University computer science professor Edward Felten and co-authors caused them to withdraw from a conference a paper they had written about issues with DRM for digital music; see *Princeton Scientists Sue Over Squelched Research* (EFF 2011a).
- At the request of Blackboard, Inc., a court in Georgia issued an injunction forbidding a student presentation at the InterzOne conference in Atlanta in 2003 on security flaws in some Blackboard software (see Borland 2003)

(although we should clarify that the DMCA was only mentioned in Blackboard's initial cease-and-desist letter, not the later legal proceedings).

Generally, §1201 has had a chilling effect on academic free speech[6] on certain topics. We have seen examples of its effect on security research—even President George W. Bush's Cybersecurity Czar Richard Clarke said that the DMCA needs reform for this reason: "I think a lot of people didn't realize that it would have this potential chilling effect on vulnerability research" (Bray 2002).

Another innovation in the DMCA is a safe harbor provision §512 that protects Internet media distribution services like YouTube against litigation for so long as they attempt to respect copyrights. One required action to earn this protection is the "notice and takedown" process, the results of which Internet users see so frequently when unable to find some audio or video they want. There are also examples of §512 being misused, such as politicians or corporations using bogus copyright infringement notices to force YouTube to take down critical videos and even to shut down the accounts originating the criticism after repeated notices. The Electronic Frontier Foundation (EFF) maintains a page called *Takedown Hall of Shame* at eff. org/takedowns, listing the worst of such spurious takedowns.[7]

From Copyright to Copyleft and FLOSS

There is a small technical point we mentioned when discussing DRM which has enormous consequences. We said that a programmer could tinker with the software on a machine and copy digital content, whether it is a download or claims to be a live stream. This is completely trivial without DRM and of varying difficulty—from easy to hard, but in practice never impossible—with DRM. That is, you can make a copy *if* your machine does what you tell it to, runs the programs you want, and doesn't lie to you when you ask its operating system to tell you about hardware and software resources. HAL 9000 and Frankenstein's monster can make circumventing DRM impossible, but a universal Turing machine[8] that you own and can program as you like cannot. For this reason, Cory Doctorow refers to the digital media middleman's attempt to rule the Internet with DRM as a *war on general-purpose computing* (Doctorow 2012a).

The whole structure whereby middlemen make money by distributing digital media with DRM, which cannot be legally removed thanks to the DMCA, is based on locking down the UTMs we own. Of course, one might object that the DMCA provides a legal block to circumvention already, but experience shows that digital media which are popular on a mass scale get so much attention—think of this as the teen-age cracker[9] version of the infinite number of monkeys who write *Hamlet*—that the DRM is quickly removed and the media are posted on file-sharing sites, despite the legal prohibition. At that point, the ethical standards felt by millions of users regarding downloading *just one more* song (video, e-book, video game, etc.) mean the profit stream of the middlemen may be seriously compromised.

In short, there is a fierce financial motivation for hardware manufacturers to constrain what software can run on their machines, which we should think of as de-universalizing a UTM, and commercial software vendors who provide everything from operating systems to video playback software to prevent the user and owner of a computer from fully controlling it. The hardware approach has, fortunately, been fairly slow. In the PC market, it involves a bit of extra hardware in the device called a Trusted Platform Module (TPM), which supports something called *secure boot* (although *restricted boot* would be a more accurate term). On the software level, just about all commercial software participates in this project of controlling users. Operating systems like Windows and OS X, players like Adobe Acrobat, and the Flash plugin, many hardware drivers running under any operating system, are all actually working for their corporate authors, not the consumer who runs them.

There is good news (on the software front at least): there is an excellent alternative, which keeps consumers in control of their own powerful UTMs. This alternative is *free software*.

This term does not refer to the cost of the software. English lacks a distinction between *free* meaning *costs nothing* and *free* meaning *unrestricted* or *not under someone else's control*, but many other languages do have this distinction: *gratis, gratuit,* and *kostenlos* mean *costs nothing* in Italian, French, and German, respectively, while *libero, libre,* and *frei* mean *unrestricted* in the same languages. The kind of freedom we mean when talking about software is the one that has to do with lack of restrictions, not lack of cost. "'Free' as in 'free speech,' not as in 'free beer,'" Richard M. Stallman defined it (Stallman, et al. 2002), around the time he started the Free Software Foundation (FSF) in the mid-1980s.

Another term more frequently used today than *free software* is *open-source software*, but this is actually a mistake, as Stallman pointed out some time ago (Stallman et al. 2002). The idea of *open source* is that the users are able to look at the source code of the programs they run. *Source code* is the version of the program that a human wrote, in some language like **Java** or **C++** and that can be read, and modified, by another human being. This is not true for the *executable*, which is what the computer itself needs in order to execute the program but which looks like complete gibberish to humans. Commercial software is usually distributed in executable form only, which means that the user cannot read the code, cannot learn from the techniques it uses, and cannot modify it or customize it to their own specialized uses.[10]

Therefore, having the source code of a program is a necessary (without de-compilers) condition for tinkering with that program, but it is not sufficient. There may be legal barriers, such as intellectual property law and license terms, to doing whatever some user wants to do with the program. After all, the source code of a book is the human-readable words on its pages and yet copyright law restricts what we can legally do with books (publish our own editions, write sequels, etc.) without the permission of the copyright holder, despite always having the source code.

To call a piece of software *open source* means to emphasize its technical readiness to be cracked, not its availability for tinkering, learning, and adaptation. To emphasize those freedoms, regardless of whether the source code is public or not, we should call it *free software*—although it would be silly for a programmer to give the public freedom to tinker with one of his or her programs without making it easy by making the source code public as well, so in practice, all free software is open source.

One strategy to deal with this terminological confusion is to combine a term for freedom with another from a different language. This second term has the crucial distinction between no cost and no restrictions. Put them together and the result is *free/libre/open-source software*. While this is quite a mouthful, at least it has a nice acronym, FLOSS.

Richard Stallman, as a founding demiurge of the free software movement, codified all of this in the following definition (Stallman et al. 2002):

A program is free software if the program's users have the four essential freedoms:

- The freedom to run the program as you wish, for any purpose (freedom 0).
- The freedom to study how the program works, and change it so it does your computing as you wish (freedom 1). Access to the source code is a precondition for this.
- The freedom to redistribute copies so you can help your neighbors (freedom 2).
- The freedom to distribute copies of your modified versions to others (freedom 3). By doing this your can give the whole community a chance to benefit from your changes. Access to the source code is a precondition for this.

Stallman then took the idea of free software one step further. You can look for freedom for yourself to tinker with a program, but if you take a great piece of free software, tinker, and then put it out in the world (presumably by selling it) in a nonfree form, then the community has lost something. So to make free software into a common good, we should release our software not only as free, but with a sort of self-replicating legal attachment that requires that any descendant works, modified or not, must also be free, and must as well carry this replication clause.[11] He named this concept *copyleft*, in order to make explicit the contrast with copyright. In consultation with legal experts, the idea of copyleft was encoded in a license, now in its third iteration, the *GNU Public License (GPL)*.

The word *GNU* in that name stands for *GNU's Not Unix*, in a self-referential (really, recursive) definition that mentions the great operating system Unix, which was widely used by sophisticated computer users after its development at Bell Labs in the 1970s. Stallman founded something he called the *GNU Project* around the same time as the FSF, whose goal was to produce software that will be widely useful. A very large part of the software in the operating system usually known as Linux is GNU software, so that in fact it should really be called GNU/Linux.

FLOSS and Higher Education

There seems to be something very familiar in the four essential freedoms that Richard Stallman stated for free software, apart from the legal technicalities of copyright and the unfolding historical drama in the modern history of software. Just look at the *1940 Statement of Principles on Academic Freedom and Tenure* (AAUP 1940), in which the American Association of University Professors elaborated upon its definition of the term *academic freedom*.

> Institutions of higher education are conducted for the common good and not to further the interest of either the individual teacher or the institution as a whole. The common good depends upon the free search for truth and its free exposition.
>
> Academic freedom is essential to these purposes and applies to both teaching and research. Freedom in research is fundamental to the advancement of truth. Academic freedom in its teaching aspect is fundamental for the protection of the rights of the teacher in teaching and of the student to freedom in learning. It carries with it duties correlative with rights.

Later in the *1940 Statement*, the AAUP gives more precise details about the specific tenets of academic freedom, covering rights and responsibilities for research, classroom teaching, and extramural communications. The AAUP statement serves as a bulwark against forces within universities that control the actions of its scholars, limiting their freedom to take their research wherever it leads or to share their discoveries however they deem best in the classroom and to the wider world.

EULAs and nonfree software are antithetical to the ways the scholarly life is practiced—at least today, in non-profit universities. If a program was used in an institution of higher education and a scholar wanted to change its functionality for his or her research, to use it in an unexpected way for their teaching, or to share with other scholars and students, and this were disallowed because of failure of the four fundamental software freedoms, that would surely constitute a failure of academic freedom. This means that any piece of nonfree software used at a university is a failure of academic freedom simply waiting to happen, waiting for the first truly innovative teacher or researcher.

For example, if an authority figure at a university were to come to a classroom and start to prescribe which color chalk or markers to use for which parts of a lecture or how many minutes to spend on which kinds of classroom activity, or that only multiple-choice quizzes could be given, the faculty would laugh and confidently assert primacy over those kinds of decisions. Similarly, if an authority figure told a laboratory scientist that he or she could only use reagents from one particular company in their experiments, or if a social scientist were told they could only use books and journals published by one particular publishing firm with which their university had made an agreement, again these scholars would laugh and insist otherwise. Yet somehow, when university administrations and business offices make deals which are much more restrictive with software and IT service vendors, faculty do not perceive it as a matter of academic freedom.

Actually, the idea of free software and copyleft echoes much older and more fundamental ideas—the application to the realm of software of the project of the scholarly life which threads through the Enlightenment, the Scientific Method, and even predates Plato's Academy; this is probably perfectly obvious to any faculty member, but let us follow that thread just a little.

Scientific papers today have a fairly tediously repetitive style. They all have a *title, abstract, introduction, methods, results, discussion,* and *references.* Notice the *methods* preceding the *results:* no scientist would simply tell their results without explaining the method. The social contract of science is to tell everyone how you did what you did, because only then does it have any chance of being trusted and only then will others be able to build on it—and others building on (citing) your work is the currency of success in science.

Cory Doctorow has a beautiful example (which he puts into the mouth of a character in a novel (Doctorow 2012b) and tells an interviewer in *The Guardian* (Pauli 2009)) of the difference between alchemy and chemistry being like the difference between nonfree and free software. Here is another: Almost every mathematics student knows the name of Pythagoras and his eponymous theorem—when JP asks his students to state their favorite theorem on the first day of a class, almost all say the Pythagorean Theorem, simply because that is the only theorem *with a name* that they know. But this theorem did not originate with Pythagoras, as we know it was familiar to Egyptians and Babylonians well before Pythagoras. In fact, other than some vague idea that *All is number,* most of the deep ideas of the Pythagoreans are lost. Probably this is due to the fact that Pythagoras structured his school almost like a religion (or even a cult), keeping its most important ideas secrets known only to the inner circle. There is even a probably apocryphal story that the Pythagorean follower Hippasus was murdered for revealing to the public the closely guarded secret that is $\sqrt{2}$ irrational.[12]

Contrast this with Euclid, who wrote up his *Elements,* which contained all of the theorems he knew, proved as clearly, carefully, and completely as he was able, and distributed widely. The *Elements* is estimated to have gone through more editions than any other book in the West except the Christian Bible (Boyer and Merzbach 2011). Knowledge of the *Elements* was considered basic to an educated person in a number of times and places in the last two thousand years. Kepler, Galileo, Descartes, Newton, and Einstein are just a few of the many famous scientists who told specific stories of the importance of the *Elements* in their lives. Apparently, a crucial step for real, lasting importance as a mathematician is to publish all of the *proofs* of your theorems, their *source code,* and to encourage others to use your ideas, to tinker with them, and to publish their new proofs in turn—in fact, without doing this you would not, any time in the last two thousand years,[13] be considered a mathematician at all.

Free software and copyleft are built the way professors do higher education, and to use nonfree software is to abrogate the defense of academic freedom and to invite its failure, sooner or later.

We should mention in passing that the academic freedom, which we contend is embodied by free software and threatened by the use of nonfree software in higher education, need not be any particular one of the various forms of academic freedom which are sometimes debated. In particular, Stanley Fish has a recent book (Fish 2014) in which he claims to find five schools of thought about what academic freedom really is and what its justification could be. We don't see any particular reason to engage Fish on the details of his analysis, partly because we do not agree with much of it,[14] but more importantly because we think that the above discussion is valid for any of his versions of academic freedom.

Practicalities of FLOSS

The freedom that academics enjoy to follow their research wherever it may lead and to teach their students in whichever way their professional judgement indicates always faces the very hard boundary of practicality. If a physicist feels that he or she needs to construct a multi-billion dollar particle accelerator in order to get to the next crucial data for their theory-building, or if a classicist insists that teaching the *Odyssey* must involve taking the students to Greece and sailing with them through storms and between islands, it is not a violation of academic freedom for these professors' chairs and deans simply to say "no."

All of our idealism about free software and its consonance with the scholarly project will come to nothing if there is not sufficient software to handle the IT needs of a modern university that is free and also affordable, convenient, secure, and reliable. Fortunately, such software is abundant.

Consider the operating system, GNU/Linux. There are many versions, with particular sets of pre-installed software, hence most easily used for particular applications. These versions are called *distributions*, and they include Linux Mint, Ubuntu, Debian, openSUSE, Fedora, and around six hundred others (according to *The LWN.net Linux Distribution List*).

Running under GNU/Linux is FLOSS for office applications, scientific work, business needs, audio and video editing and playback, most programming languages, typesetting (including difficult scientific and mathematical), encryption, games, and so on. There are educational applications such as homework systems with automated grading, learning management systems, student records and financial tracking, and library management. There are Internet services such as wiki engines, blogging and forum software, web servers and browsers.

The way to think of the FLOSS ecosystem is by analogy with the collective output of the world's scholarship, since FLOSS is the software analogue of the scholarly project. Today, if we wanted to understand a scholarly question, we would go to our favorite search engine and look for papers with certain keywords, and we would almost always get many hits—from many thousands for questions of wide interest to just a few to hard questions which few have made much progress on (and rarely zero: zero hits means someone should work on that problem!). Similarly, for a task we want to do in the IT world, going to a search engine yields from a few to a very large number of FLOSS solutions, with many variations and specializations.

Furthermore, just as a result in physical science is refined as new experiments change some of our understanding of the phenomena, so do flaws or gaps in existing FLOSS projects tend to get fixed more quickly and effectively than in nonfree software. The adage in the FLOSS community is *With enough eyeballs, all bugs are shallow*. This does not mean that all FLOSS projects are bug-free. Why should it? The history of science is filled with theories that were widely believed but later were modified, and so it goes with FLOSS. But, in the end, we see time and again that science is better than the alternative. In the same way, and for exactly the same reasons, FLOSS tends to be of much higher quality, and to have fewer security problems, in particular. As one example, there are hundreds of thousands or perhaps millions of viruses circulating for the most common nonfree operating system, while there might be two dozen for GNU/Linux.

Another practical issue is simply to convince university faculty and staff to try FLOSS. Often they (particularly staff) are worried about what they will do if something goes wrong—the *"Who you gonna call?"* problem. But, as we have said, FLOSS is more reliable than nonfree software. And the corporate helpdesks frequently aren't actually helpful. The actual downtime on our campus for large, critical IT systems—which were nonfree and under service contracts —in the last few years has been a scandal, as it often is on university campuses.

You might wonder what professor has the time to learn something new. After all, many professors are already both over-worked and have something which they know will work even if that something is far from perfect. Ironically, nonfree software imposes more time-wasting and IT-learning on faculty, when the software goes into a new version or the vendor takes away a feature you like, or adds some distracting new ones. FLOSS only changes when the user wants it to, motivated by their professional judgment as scholars and teachers.

An even better answer, to both of these objections, is to ask how a faculty member would respond if a student said analogous things in a class. When a student says they were unable to finish an assignment because their tutor was unavailable, we faculty tend to respond that it is the student's responsibility to learn the material and to handle the problems on their own when necessary—no corporate helpdesks, just learn to deal with complications on your own. Likewise, if a student didn't want to learn something a little complicated but which would give them enormous new power to control their educational future, we would say that they should just learn these tools of autonomy, even if it requires a little effort.

In this context, it is hard not to hear the famous lines of Kant's *An Answer to the Question: What is Enlightenment?* (Kant 1784) as if he were speaking directly about free software:

Enlightenment is man's emergence from his self-imposed immaturity. Immaturity is the inability to use one's understanding without guidance from another. This immaturity is self-imposed when its cause lies not in lack of understanding, but in lack of resolve and courage to use it without guidance from another. *Sapere Aude!* [dare to know] 'Have courage to use your own understanding!' that is the motto of enlightenment.

Laziness and cowardice are the reasons why so great a proportion of men, long after nature has released them from alien guidance (*naturaliter maiorennes*), nonetheless gladly remain in lifelong immaturity, and why it is so easy for others to establish themselves as their guardians. It is so easy to be immature.

We should not expect to be able to teach our students autonomy and agency and to stand up for their rights in society if we have given up our own autonomy and agency. We should not accept numerous violations of our academic freedom (remember, every time we are told "the system can't do that," it is a failure of academic freedom), because we are too lazy to learn something new and lack the courage to stand up for the freedom to choose the (entirely reasonable and practical) tools we want for our research and teaching.

Notes

1 In the sense of *those who like John Locke, Adam Smith, and John Stuart Mill*, not in the sense with which that word is used in today's American or UK politics.
2 However, this does seem to be a very modern issue, since it relies upon the extremely small marginal cost of distributing digital media in the Internet Age, so we should not fault the Founders for not foreseeing it.
3 This is already a bit weird, in a certain sense, since only a small portion of the huge profits they made was shared with the actual creators. Nevertheless, it was asserted that there was no point in arguing with what was actually happening on the ground, and cutting those profits to the middlemen would mean *nothing* would get to the artists.
4 Recall a *bit* is the smallest unit of information: a value which can be either 0 or 1. The term was invented by the great statistician John Tukey—who also coined the term *software*—as a shortened form for *binary digit*, meaning a digit of a number written in base two.
5 Some say that *DRM* stands for *Digital **Rights** Management*. This version is better.
6 Implicit in DMCA §1201 is the idea that talking in public about flaw in a commercial DRM product is as dangerous as revealing national secrets or shouting *fire* in a crowded theater, and therefore does not deserve 1st Amendment protection.
7 The reader who is interested in more detail on copyright law has (too) many options. We suggest any of the books of William Patry, such as his legal textbooks on the subject and his more recent books for a general audience, *Moral Panics and the Copyright Wars* (Patry 2009) and *How to Fix Copyright* (Patry 2012).
8 Recall our previous, quite informal definition of a universal Turing machine (UTM) as an idealized model of a device that can perform any computation which can be clearly stated as an algorithm.
9 Among IT enthusiasts, a *hacker* is "a person who delights in having an intimate understanding of the internal workings of a system" (Internet User's Glossary 1993), and who delights in cleverly using that system in new, unanticipated ways, while a *cracker* is "an individual who attempts to access computer systems without authorization." We will use that better terminology, along with the verb forms *hack* and *crack*, in this book.
10 Well, there are techniques including *patching an executable* and running it through a *decompiler*, but they are extremely difficult and are mostly only used by determined crackers.

11 Detractors call this kind of self-replicating license *viral*, as if it were the software form of Ebola or some other disease.

12 Meaning that there do not exist any two whole numbers p and q such that $p / q = \sqrt{2}$. A very amusing version of the story of Hippasus of Metapontum is told in Morris (2011).

13 With the exception of a strange, non-productive period in the early sixteenth century, mostly in northern Italy.

14 A colleague of ours thinks that the arguments Fish marshals for his positions are so transparently weak that they must be a sort of poison pill intended to prove exactly the opposite of what they appear to be saying.

5

UNBUNDLING

The Flipped Classroom and Its Possible Effects

David Vanden Bout and Cynthia LaBrake were teaching Chemistry 301 together at the University of Texas at Austin. One morning in 2013, class began with a short lecture by Vanden Bout on covalent bonding. It was then followed by their students working together in small groups drawing bonds. While this happened, two graduate students and eight "peer mentors" (undergraduates who had received a grade of "B" or better) circulated between groups, helping their fellow students to understand the content (Ebbeler 2013).

Those students who had done as the syllabus required first learned about that content on something called *Quest*, which was developed by the College of Natural Sciences at UT-Austin to host online content for those classes. Quest has spread to 48 other universities and over 900 high schools across the country (College of Natural Science, University of Texas 2011). Students use Quest for two kinds of homework: Learning Modules and Homework Sets. According to Vanden Bout and LaBrake's syllabus,

> Learning Modules are designed to introduce new concepts and/or direct teach basic skills outside of class. Homework Sets are a series of problems that you should work through to help you solidify your conceptual understanding of the material and to develop more sophisticated problem-solving skills.
>
> *(Vanden Bout, et al. 2013)*

The idea behind this course design is for students to learn as much about the content as they can outside of class, so that they can spend in-class time demonstrating mastery of the content and getting help as needed.

What do the instructors do in this arrangement? Besides those short lectures, they're presumably walking around at the class at the same time that the graduate students and peer mentors are, but, more importantly, they create the content that students learn. "[Creating content ourselves] shows that we care," explained LaBrake in the *Daily Texan* (Ebbeler 2013). Creating (and owning) their content themselves also explains why the State of Texas continues to pay their salaries.

But now imagine a similar arrangement at a different kind of school. Students learn content at home, but they never meet the instructors who created that content. The instructors they do meet don't have tenure or, perhaps, any expertise in the subject which they are teaching. Nor do they have the academic freedom to determine how the courses they are teaching actually get taught. While this may seem far-fetched that was exactly the situation at San Jose State University, created when it moved Michael Sandel's *Justice* MOOC from Philosophy to English. When cash-strapped administrations realize that they can offload aspects of their faculty's jobs to the Internet and therefore pay less-qualified on-site people less, this situation is likely to become much more common.

The new buzzword for this practice is "unbundling." That's a reference to breaking something up into its constituent pieces and selling it separately. Don't want to buy the entire album? With iTunes or Amazon you can just buy individual songs. Don't want to take a foreign language class to get your university degree because you think you won't need it in your chosen field? Now MOOC providers like Coursera can offer you what some are calling "microdegrees," specialized certificates in particular fields that students can show employers. The idea here is to make the traditional university degree obsolete, at least with respect to getting a job (Butler 2015).

Because so many higher education reforms come from outside of academia, questions about the educational quality of an unbundled classroom seldom get discussed. Those classes that depend upon the transfer of information like anatomy and physiology might survive total unbundling, but not any subject requiring critical thinking, problem solving, and creativity, because those require prolonged dialogue between instructors and students in order to be taught properly. If different people are on the other end of those conversations, they are unlikely to offer students the same guidance, particularly if the criteria for evaluating success in those subjects are complex and require human judgment.

Unbundling the university degree represents a triumph of vocationalism. What happens to faculty who don't teach in vocationally-oriented disciplines under this model is seldom discussed either. Of course, they are the ones whose jobs will get disrupted. Similarly, it is likely that the Internet will increase the size of the administrative cadre in higher education going forward. Somebody will have to pay close attention to all the new activities that digitalization lets administrators monitor, such as the day-to-day activities in individual classes.

Professors ought to be wary of having their jobs broken into pieces since they may not be able to put all those pieces back together again. Yet Professors Vanden Bout and LaBrake, for example, have in essence unbundled themselves. As Ryan

Craig advocates in his book *College Disrupted*, "Disaggregate the role of faculty to achieve development and delivery efficiencies. Specialist faculty will develop courses. Different faculty will provide instruction. Another group will provide assessment services. Yet another will handle advisement and support" (Craig 2015). At an abstract level, there is no difference between what Craig is proposing here and what Henry Ford did for auto assembly workers about a hundred years ago, except Ford gave his employees a big raise so that they'd be more likely to tolerate their newly uninspiring work pattern. Also, of course, teaching real live human beings is not at all like building a car.

Those faculty members who do unbundle themselves may have ample pedagogical reasons for doing so, but they do not unbundle in a vacuum. Any faculty member who doesn't create their own content runs the risk of having that aspect of their job performed by others, especially if they do not have tenure to protect them. Other aspects of faculty jobs like grading and advising are already getting unbundled so that they can be performed by computers. While professors everywhere may welcome relief from some of these onerous responsibilities, they might also consider being careful what they wish for because the responsibilities that form the basis of their duties can be unbundled too. Should you choose to unbundle yourself, our advice is that you make sure that you have absolute control over the content that you use. The fact that any class could be unbundled involuntarily is a threat to professors' prerogatives in classes of all kinds.

Flipped classrooms are perhaps the best-known example of unbundling today. Like Professors Vanden Bout and LaBrake's chemistry class, this strategy involves students learning content outside of class so that they can concentrate on mastery in class. But almost any humanities class, like history or English, would count as flipped under this definition. Flipping has taken on a new meaning since the introduction of Salman Khan's Khan Academy in 2006. Nowadays, flipped classes often involve gaining content knowledge through Internet video. In secondary schools, where Khan Academy has thrived, that content never involves a student's teacher being the one to impart that knowledge. Many universities have been experimenting with something called "lecture capture" so professors can essentially flip themselves. MOOC lectures have also become an important potential product for flipped classrooms well beyond the hallowed halls of the august universities that produce such classes.

Proponents of flipped classrooms justify them by noting the ways that it frees up class time for direct interaction between faculty and individual students. This makes sense in classes that are small or which have teaching assistants or paid student mentors to help students who are struggling with the course materials. It does not make sense in classes that depend upon reading assignments, since few students would be willing to read a novel or a textbook *and* then watch videos about the same material before class even starts as many of them have jobs or other aspects of life to live.

Some classes—particularly outside the humanities—might benefit from adopting this practice. In large lecture halls, even the small amount of faculty–student interaction that flipping the classroom might create would be an improvement over the passive learning that dominates there. While these pedagogical objections to flipped classrooms may not apply to chemistry professors, flipping your classroom never occurs without context. In an environment where faculty are politically unpopular and there are plenty of technological alternatives to traditional classroom teaching being developed by profit-hungry edtech entrepreneurs, the employment-related implications of classroom flipping need to be fully appreciated.

Indeed, flipped classrooms are symptomatic of a larger problem in the dysfunctional relationship between higher education and the Internet: the temptation of faculty to offload their duties to the World Wide Web. In the name of efficiency, convenience, data collection, or perhaps simple laziness, professors are using the Internet, in general, and the flipped classroom technique, in particular, to unbundle themselves. While that might not be such a bad thing for those faculty members who can control all the conditions of their employment, most faculty can't. While these technological objects may not apply to tenured professors at universities like UT-Austin, the employment-related implications of flipped classrooms deserve serious consideration by any potential classroom flipper in a professionally precarious position.

Under these circumstances, administrators could easily use the content they buy from MOOC providers, or elsewhere, to replace existing faculty whether they actually flip their classrooms or not. Steven Mintz, who runs the University of Texas System's Institute for Transformational Learning, has suggested that MOOC providers, in order to rejuvenate their business models, could "disaggregate course content and make the assets available to any faculty member (or institution) to use" (Mintz 2015). Translated, that means that the faculty who use MOOC lectures could see their courses flipped involuntarily, their classes turned into discrete bits of content, with that content flowing according to the whims of others. In fact, even faculty who simply tape themselves could end up having their work resold without compensation or control, depending upon campus policies about copyright ownership (see the discussion in Chapter 8 on *works for hire*). Teachers, like artists, ought to be wary of letting others dictate how their work is distributed.

When you outsource content provision to the Internet, you put yourself in competition with it—and it is very hard to compete with the Internet. After all, if you aren't the best lecturer in the world, why shouldn't your boss replace you with whoever is? If other students can answer all the questions that the most confused pupils face, why not let them? If other students can actually grade papers in such a way, why not let them? This will free up the professor to do the things that really matter—like have more face-to-face discussions with the most interested students. That's only true if professors control their own classrooms, and that's not always true even among professors on the tenure track.

Unbundling the teaching process changes the entire power dynamic in the classroom. When students gain unprecedented control of the learning process, it means there are fewer decisions for the professor to make. This makes him or her more of a facilitator than a professor (in the literal sense of that word, "one who professes"). Unfortunately, for faculty facing this situation, it doesn't take seven years of graduate school in order to become a facilitator. If you aren't the one providing the content, why did you spend all those years in graduate school anyway? Even if you are a great teacher, cash-strapped administrators can pay graduate students or adjuncts a lot less to do your job. Divide the job of the faculty member into discrete parts and it becomes particularly easy to find people who can do your job more efficiently for less, if that's the scenario that your university wants.

While it is easy to imagine a pedagogical justification for dividing a professor's job if you believe that teaching raw facts or mindless algorithms is the main goal of education, it is difficult to imagine anyone recommending this arrangement for every course in a university's curriculum. For example, a divided classroom would be a nightmare for those of us who devote our courses to pursuing critical thinking. Sure, you might be able to learn to do the rote symbolic manipulations of algebra by watching videos and doing worksheets in class, but it's very unlikely that you'll ever understand why the right answer is right, how to use a technique in a new situation, or what it really means, unless you can directly engage with an instructor. If your instructor is too busy helping a hundred other people understand how to complete their worksheets, then that is very unlikely ever to happen.

Whether or not you flip your classroom every faculty member ought to support the choice of every other faculty member to make that decision for themselves. That's why warning bells should go off when a vice-chancellor at the University of Adelaide in Australia openly declares that lectures are obsolete. That was the justification for the entire school to begin to phase out lectures, instead imposing flipped classrooms on the whole university at once—citing increased retention and student satisfaction as their justification (Dodd 2015b). So thanks to the Internet, what was once the exclusive province of the faculty has become just another aspect of the university experience for administrators to manage. This isn't good for faculty certainly, but it's also terrible for the overall quality of education. The easiest way to keep every student satisfied would be to award them all "A"s on the first day and send them home.

An Automated Education Is a Contradiction in Terms

Grading is certainly the most onerous task that faculty have to perform when doing their jobs (with the possible exception of attending meetings). Assuming grades have to be awarded on the basis of work instead of just for showing up, the question becomes who gets to do the grading. Wouldn't it be great if machines could do that job for us? Of course, in classes where multiple-choice answers are considered acceptable, they already do. But for other classes and disciplines where work does not only have a finite set of alternatives as possible answers, there has been a substantial amount of research done on machine grading in recent years. MOOC providers, who have many students and no desire to pay people to read anything, have been huge backers of these efforts (Markoff 2013).

Unfortunately, these kinds of software packages can't grade on style. As one commentator on a *New York Times* article on this subject explained,

> Last year when my daughter was in 7th grade, her teacher started using computer essay grading. She would write her essay at home, using the computer, and would get a score. My daughter loves to write but got frustrated because the computer insisted on correcting the grammatical errors of portions of the essay in which she used poetic language. In order to get a higher score, she begrudgingly changed her essay.
>
> *(Markoff 2013)*

They also have a problem in evaluating the accuracy of historical facts. In other words, they can't tell whether the War of 1812 started in 1812 or 1945 (Winerip 2012).

Of course, it's likely that these problems with computer grading software will be worked out eventually. Connecting a machine grading program to the fact-checking capabilities of the Internet in general can't be *that* hard. However, even that kind of machine grading program would provide an inferior education. Those of us who grade essays understand that the most important kinds of learning come not in the corrections we make, but from the comments we write. The comments at the ends of essays can explain, inspire and question a student's assumptions about the world. In this way, they are like the act of teaching itself—an intensely personal endeavor that can be mimicked by robots and unqualified machine tenders, but never really duplicated.

In 2013, history professor Mark Cheathem participated in a conference call with a big textbook publisher. That publisher had created an enormous number of features to go with the newest version of a new publication, but the feature that attracted the most attention was the ability to grade essays automatically. Some professors, particularly those with large classes, thought this was a terrific idea, as it would save them an enormous amount of time. Others were convinced that employing this particular tool was "tantamount to firing themselves." Based on this discussion, Cheathem concluded,

> Technology may be changing higher education, but there are a lot of people and companies who don't know exactly what that change is going to look like or how to use it as a tool to help faculty rather than to replace them.
>
> *(Cheathem 2013)*

That distinction brings to mind John Markoff's division between Artificial Intelligence and Intelligence Augmentation in his book, *Machines of Loving Grace*. Artificial intelligence refers to longstanding research efforts to create computers or robots that can do complex, human-like tasks on their own, such as packing a box in a warehouse, driving a car on the public roadways, or writing a poem. Intelligence augmentation, another longstanding area for research, refers to tools that help humans do their jobs better, whether that means helping astronomers and astronauts explore space or organizing all of the world's information. According to Markoff, this division has been present in computer science research of all kinds since the earliest days of these machines (Markoff 2015, xiii).

Whether the machine grading of essays falls on one side of this divide or the other depends upon the context in which this technology gets used. If a professor feels safe in his or her job, they control their own classroom and could likely introduce this technology with no fear of being forcibly unbundled. Unfortunately, very few professors should feel safe in their jobs these days. Implemented as a time-saving measure, professors can go back and check grades which cause students to have questions. Implemented as a labor-saving measure, it will be hard for students to find anybody at all who has the power to change their grade. Such are the effects of aggressive unbundling.

ELIZA was a computer program written by Joseph Weizenbaum of MIT between 1964 and 1966 that simulated a psychotherapy session. Type a question into the program, and ELIZA would create another question based upon the language in the original question. For example, if you wrote something along the lines of "My mother is making me angry," the computer might respond with "Tell me more about your mother." Despite ELIZA's simplicity, people using it tended to quickly get entranced by the opportunity to talk about themselves. Weizenbaum himself was deeply concerned that people were being fooled into thinking that the machine actually cared about them (Turkle 2011, 23–24).

Computers have gotten a lot faster and programs much more sophisticated since the 1960s. As a result, the kinds of conversations that programs like ELIZA—which are called *chatbots*—can carry out have gotten more sophisticated too. "The holy grail of learning is personalized or adaptive learning," explained Anant Agarwal of edX in April 2015.

> This form of learning is what you might experience from an excellent personal tutor who is able to tailor your individual experience. In many ways, adaptive learning can be compared with those old 'Choose Your Own Adventure' books. At each step in the learning process, the user is given multiple options that satisfy his or her level of comprehension, style or direction. They may all lead to the same place (mastery of the material). but the path can be very different and structured for a particular learner.
>
> *(Agarwal 2015a)*

While Agarwal mentioned this in the context of edX's MOOCs, there's no reason that this technology has to be scaled to thousands of people at once. It would, at least in theory, work just as well with twenty students as it would with twenty thousand.

The first signs of automated education are easily visible to anyone who reads the higher education press. For example, Arizona State University (ASU) currently enrolls most of its undergraduates in math classes run primarily by computers. "Having a computer for an instructor was a change for [student Arnecia] Hawkins," explains a 2013 story in *Scientific American* about the experiment.

> 'I'm not gonna lie – at first I was really annoyed with it,' she says. The arrangement was a switch for her professor, too. David Heckman, a mathematician,

was accustomed to lecturing to the class, but he had to take on the role of a roving mentor, responding to raised hands and coaching students when they got stumped.

(Fletcher 2013)

If the computer program is effective, what's to stop Arizona State from removing Professor Heckman entirely? Not much. Many of the math sections at ASU already have a student-faculty ratio of 100:1 (Warner 2014). For most of those students, he might as well be gone already.

What makes this situation possible is an approach to instruction that favors content knowledge over any kind of critical thinking skills. As the author of that Arizona State article concludes, "Sufficiently advanced testing is indistinguishable from instruction" (Fletcher 2013, 5). Indeed, many competency-based education programs—new efforts being implemented across the United States to certify students for skills that they already have—employ no instructors at all (Watters 2014b). Do nothing, and whole universities without professors of any kind, and also without any education in critical thinking, are pretty much inevitable.

Most university presidents, however, won't admit this directly. "There's a tsunami coming," John Hennessy of Stanford told *The New Yorker* in 2012 (Auletta 2012). That presumably explains his efforts to keep his university at the forefront of the educational technology revolution. It is better to ride the wave than to be submerged by it. Yet the whole metaphor, even the construction of the sentence by which Hennessy presents it, paints him as a passive actor. He is not leading a revolution, but following a movement that would occur whether Stanford involved itself with education technology or not.

Elsewhere, Hennessy has spoken frankly about the effects of this "tsunami" on universities in general and the professoriate in particular. At a 2012 forum on "Higher Education in the Digital Age," Hennessy declared that the public university model is untenable. Therefore, "You just have to blow up the system" (Cicero 2012). More importantly for purposes of this analysis, he told the gathering that "faculties will shrink as technologies grow" (Bowen 2015b). The author Kevin Carey is only slightly more circumspect. Faced with the advent of the University of Everywhere, an open educational system enabled by the Internet and bound to no particular place, he admits in *The End of College* that where scholars currently earning their living from the tuition and fees of paying students "will go and how they will support themselves are today questions that have no easy answers" (Carey 2015). Stanford, where direct contact with a world-class faculty comes at a hefty price, will be likely to continue to employ humanities professors for the foreseeable future, but if this wave goes unchecked a lot of professors who are currently employed elsewhere will inevitably be displaced by technology.

Of course, this kind of advocate of technology in the classroom will tell you that it is not intended to replace teachers. In an *Inside Higher Education* article about work being done at the University of Wisconsin – Madison on what researchers there have dubbed "machine teaching," one of the principle investigators told the reporter "this will not minimize the teacher or faculty member role, but would help to optimize the teacher's time, so he or she could spend the least amount of time necessary on a subject before every student fully understood it" (Thomsen 2015). Unfortunately, the professors who develop this technology have no power over exactly how it gets employed—especially if it ever gets licensed by private companies. Arguing that automation will free up workers to concentrate on more meaningful work is a common argument in Silicon Valley. As the critic Nicholas Carr explains, "high-flown rhetoric about using technology to liberate workers of masks contempt for labor" (Carr 2014, 227).

But look at this situation from an administrator's point of view. If they buy (license) these expensive computer programs, where will they get the money to pay for them? At cash-strapped schools the inevitable justification will be because it can save labor costs: profit without workers, again. Computerized teachers, computerized scoring—these days computers will even tell students whether they're on the most efficient path towards graduation, thereby eliminating the need for advisors. Sometimes it seems as if every aspect of modern universities that can be mechanized has been mechanized. Why would actual teaching be any different?

Making this kind of switch depends upon advocates of technology changing the definition of what education is. The classes we attended at university depended upon prolonged interaction between the instructor and the students. Even in the largest of these classes, professors took questions before, during and after their lectures. If we were feeling shy, there was ample opportunity to visit professors or our teaching assistants in office hours to work through whatever problems we had in the material. Our papers were graded by human beings who explained why we earned the grades we did. It is through these kinds of exchanges that the most intense learning happens, where habits of mind are set and where inclinations develop into skills that students can employ not just in other classes, but for the rest of their lives (long after they've forgotten what their undergraduate professors' names happened to be).

The most important reason to unbundle a professor's job is to increase efficiency. After all, the pitch goes, if you can spend less time doing things that others can do better (like lecture), you can spend more time helping students learn. Unfortunately, like Lucy and Ethel in that chocolate factory back in the 1950s, it is easy for your employers to speed up your line by giving you more students—particularly if you work in an online setting where the size of the classroom is no longer a limiting factor. In this way, unbundling the professor's job limits the contact between the student and their instructor. By limiting the contact between students and their instructor, unbundled classes have to focus on how much content a student remembers rather than the kinds of skills that they develop. Anyone who really cares about teaching should consider that outcome shameful.

Other Threats to Faculty Prerogatives

One way around the need to unbundle faculty is indeed to get rid of them entirely. A popular way to do this is to award credit not for the exact number of hours that students sit in class, but for competencies that they already happen to possess. "As all employers know," explained one Canadian higher education columnist in 2012, "the average BA doesn't certify that the degree-holder actually knows anything. It merely certifies that she had the perseverance to pass the required number of courses." That's why online schools like Western Governors University (WGU) pioneered the awarding of credit through competency rather than by seat time. Give students a test before they start a course. Direct them to resources they can use to learn more. Give them a test at the end, and award credit on that basis (Wente 2012). Recently, more conventional schools like the University of Wisconsin and Kentucky's Community College System have been experimenting with such programs (Fain 2014).

Problems with these kinds of programs from the standpoint of faculty should be obvious. On a purely self-interested level, competency-based education programs don't require faculty at all—just test makers and proctors in order to monitor them. Western Governors University, for example, employs no traditional faculty. The curriculum is determined entirely by outside experts. The actual teaching duties are left to "mentors" who handle eighty students at a time, calling them up weekly in order to check on student progress (Lewin 2011). In other words, students are left essentially to teach themselves.

While WGU's mentors may have graduate degrees, they aren't exactly treated like professionals. For example, as the author of the blog "Fed Up at WGU" explained the story of a fellow mentor there:

> The students didn't have to return her calls or complete any school work. If she tried to push them at all, they would just ask to be moved to another mentor and it would be approved. Honestly, not only would it be approved, but she would be punished for their request. I told her she was giving up her life (20+) hours per week and her moral beliefs for nothing in return – not for her benefit nor for the students. The only people benefiting were her manager and WGU.
>
> *(fedupatwgu 2012)*

Having no control over curriculum or working hours or even the technology with which you interact with students is what makes this kind of treatment possible. To be unbundled this way destroys professorial power and prerogatives.

Sebastian Thrun of Udacity has called his MOOC platform an "Uber for Education," referring to the influential ridesharing service that has gone a long way towards displacing taxi drivers in major cities around the world. "With Uber any normal person with a car can become a driver," he told the *MIT Technology Review* in 2015, "and with Udacity now every person with a computer can become a global code reviewer" (Byrnes 2015). Even more than Uber, Udacity and schools like WGU can essentially crowd-source instruction to anyone with a few skills at the end of an Internet connection rather than be limited by the locality where people want rides. This gives them an enormous amount of power vis-à-vis their mentors, who have far fewer skills than traditional faculty because they need far fewer when they are only performing a small part of a traditional faculty member's job. This situation makes them all easy to replace should they ask for more autonomy—or even a little more money per course.

As bad as that situation may be for instructors, it is also possible for competency-based education to reject faculty entirely by automating the unbundled parts of teaching that can be automated. Besides employing essay-grading programs, universities could conceivably make plenty of money giving students access to warmed-over MOOC videos and charging them to take tests once students have finished viewing them. This is what we call in American football "moving the goalposts." If the idea of universal university education doesn't work for everyone, then claim that that wasn't the original goal. Plenty of universities all around the world will be very anxious to treat "competencies" gained through MOOCs as the exact same thing as having attended university because they are desperate to shed faculty labor costs, even though the faculty they want to shed are what make a university education valuable in the first place.

Whether parents and tuition-paying adult students will willingly pay thousands upon thousands of dollars to have their children's "competencies" tested is open to question. So too is whether employers hire "graduates" whose sole means of demonstrating those supposed skills is a standardized test or a MOOC completion certificate. "Do we want students to simply get through our curriculum?" asks Katherine D. Harris, "Or do we want them to learn?" (Harris 2013) This is so obvious that it shouldn't require stating, but faculty members are the best people in a university to judge learning because they are the ones who understand their own disciplines. They can also judge whether students possess certain skills by seeing them employ those skills in class rather than from taking a standardized test. Disrupt faculty by unbundling their job and these advantages disappear.

Unfortunately, whether faculty get to use their knowledge and expertise to judge what and whether students learn is threatened by the rise of a new class of administrative staff on campuses everywhere: "teaching and learning specialists." While a typical face-to-face course, or even a regular fully-online course, does not have to cater to the recommendations of the nineteen or twenty people who may collaborate to produce a MOOC, the rise of online tools has meant that professors of all kinds have less say over their own classrooms than they did even twenty years ago. One reason that the power of these staffers has increased is that the power of faculty has dwindled as technology has made it easier for faculty prerogatives to be divided when the work of teaching gets unbundled.

Who can object to more help for faculty who are interested in improving teaching and learning? We certainly don't. The problem with some approaches to this help is that they are being used to create online initiatives that bypass faculty's traditional role in major teaching-related decisions on campus. As Jefferey R. Young of the *Chronicle of Higher Education* explained in late 2015,

> [S]upporting teaching with technology is becoming less about offering training sessions for professors about how to use clickers and course-management

systems, and more about coordinating bigger-impact projects like redesigning large introductory courses or leading the creation of a new online-degree program.

Moreover, these new initiatives are often accompanied by new mid-level administrators designed to spearhead "academic-change initiatives" rather than coming up through the faculty (Young 2015).

Through such initiatives, education specialists manage to impose a new set of criteria to determine student success. Those criteria often depend upon the results of standardized tests. How can you measure learning without breaking it down into measurable chunks that render broader goals, like critical thinking, totally irrelevant? How can you measure student engagement with material on a numerical scale?[1] We believe that it is better to trust teachers to know when their methods are working, and by that we don't mean every teacher judges their own work. We mean that the best standards of success are standards determined by faculty who are experts in the disciplines that they're evaluating, not outsiders like administrators or corporate disruptors with a financial interest in finding failure everywhere they look.

To systematize and standardize learning by favoring discrete and measurable outcomes threatens the ability of faculty to express their individuality as teachers and to miss a wonderful opportunity to teach students about the world. Real life is chaotic. The World Wide Web is chaotic. Innovative online instructors can teach practical web skills along with their original disciplines as long as they have enough control over the design of their classes to work those possibilities into their syllabi and lesson plans. These same instructors can also fight back against the incessant clamor to measure the success of classes only by test scores geared to accumulating knowledge rather than skills.

Of course, plenty of instructional designers and teaching and learning professionals agree with these goals. Rather than competitors, these colleagues can become invaluable resources to interested faculty as long as they recognize the central place of professors in any college or university setting. Unless they hold dual roles on the faculty, teaching and learning professionals are not eligible for tenure. They are not in the best position to stick up for education during times of budgetary crises because they are not in the best position to speak about their true beliefs because they fear the consequences of offending those in authority. In an environment where technological infrastructure is becoming increasingly important to the success of universities everywhere, maintaining shared governance with respect to these issues is vital to every university's future.

The technological realm is also an obvious place for a university's educational mission to get in the way of the need for that institution to maintain its bottom line. So many great resources on the Internet are available for free that it is only logical to suggest that online courses could or should be the same way. Openness is also an idea that appeals to many faculty members, especially those of us who are concerned about the costs that our students have to pay for textbooks each semester. Unfortunately, these kinds of issues cannot be separated from the power relationship between faculty and administration that affects so many issues related to technology and education.

Note

1 Indeed, one of us has actually seen a proposed study that records student brain waves in order to measure engagement.

6

ELECTRONIC TAYLORISM

Progress in the Art of Sweating

Frederick Winslow Taylor was a management consultant during the late-nineteenth and early-twentieth centuries who is best known today for his theory of *scientific management* or simply *Taylorism*. While this practice is best known for its effects upon how goods are manufactured, it also has a wider reach. In the Internet Age, scientific management has even come to universities, thanks to information technology.

The simplified image we tend to have of Taylorism is of an observer with a clipboard and stopwatch. Taylor's consulting gigs also involved a lot of specialized forms to be carefully filled in and a slide rule to be furiously slid, but Taylor actually wanted an entirely new conception of the role of management, and of the attitudes of workers and managers alike. His early working life in manufacturing, including at Bethlehem Steel, occurred at a moment in American development when industrial work was moving from *craft production* to *mass production*.

The gradually fading older system was built on craft workers (artisans) who had personal skill, knowledge, and experience which they used to figure out for themselves how to accomplish their tasks. The new system was designed to function more efficiently and profitably with more modern industries where there was insufficient time for workers to get this personal expertise or knowledge of the rapidly developing new technologies; nor was it desirable (to capital – the owners and upper managers) to give them the concomitant authority and control.

That's why the principles of scientific management (in fact, a phrase that was the name of his book (Taylor 1914)), according to Taylor, were that[1]:

(1) great attention must be paid to the actions of the individual workers;
(2) a complete division must be made between the planning, to be done by professional engineers in their roles as lower and middle managers, from execution,

to be performed by the workers exactly in accordance with the detailed plans of management;

(3) every single tiniest step of the workers' activity should be carefully timed and organized; and

(4) workers should be paid a differential piece-rate, higher or lower depending upon their adherence to management's careful plans and their corresponding measured productivity.

Taylor's scientific management had an enormous impact on the development of industry in the United States, and even in Europe and farther east. None other than V.I. Lenin wrote quite a bit about it, saying for example that,

> The Taylor system, the last word of capitalism in this respect, like all capitalist progress, is a combination of the refined brutality of bourgeois exploitation and a number of the greatest scientific achievements in the field of analyzing mechanical motions during work, the elimination of superfluous and awkward motions, the elaboration of correct methods of work, the introduction of the best system of accounting and control, *etc.* The Soviet Republic must at all costs adopt all that is valuable in the achievements of science and technology in this field.
>
> *(Lenin 1972)*

(In another essay entirely about Taylorism, Lenin added that, "In capitalist society, progress in science and technology means progress in the art of sweating." (Lenin 1975))

Certainly Lenin had picked up on a very visible part of Taylorism, its time-and-motion studies (that clipboard and stopwatch), collecting information for principle (3), above, in the service of principle (2). This particular practice is just one example of the larger idea of Taylor to *deskill* workers, to take away all of the knowledge, insight, and experience of the (formerly) craft laborers and instead to invest the knowledge and insight in the professional managers.

Taylorism was useful in some measure because of the increased production it was able to get out of workers, but probably more because of its practical and philosophical revision of the role of labor. Judith Merkle argues that:

> The core of Taylorism was clearly an explicit call for reconciliation between capital and labor, on the neutral ground of science and rationality. The bribe was higher productivity, by as yet to be discovered means. Science would replace the old relations of tyranny and resistance in industrial society – but the reconciliation, quite obviously. was to be made on the terms of neither party, but in terms of 'rationality' *as interpreted by Taylor himself.* That is, power in the production process was to be transferred to the hands of those custodians who knew more about the system, and what was really good for it, through the aid of their scientific insight. In short, power would be in the

hands of Taylor, the scientific managers, and the category of well-intentioned. rational, public-spirited, virtuous, middle-class technicians that they represented. This power was the essential condition for the imposition of their world-view upon the production situation. The violent nineteenth century world of conflict between the upper and lower classes could become peaceful and productive only if it conformed to the middle-class image of reality.

(Merkle 1980)

To us, this description of labor relations and Taylor's principles of scientific management seem to describe nearly perfectly much of the organization of modern higher education (and in fact other levels of the educational system and other industries as well). It's always easy to motivate academics by appealing to rationality, and since professors are aware of their own hard-won expertise, they can easily imagine that there might exist a class of "scientific managers"— deans, provosts, vice-presidents, and so on—who are "well-intentioned. rational, public-spirited, virtuous, middle-class technicians" of university administration.[2] Attempts at the deskilling implicit in Taylorism are like nineteenth-century equivalents of attempts to unbundle or automate the work of professors today. If professors can be deskilled, they can all be replaced by adjuncts who are cheaper, fungible, and can be hired and fired with the blowing winds of demand and upper administration's strategic goals. Deskilling is supported by commercial textbooks, which are provided often with PowerPoint decks to use in class, detailed answer sheets for exercises, test banks, and online tools such as explanatory video clips, automated homework systems, and gamified electronic textbooks.

The frequent talk of *best practices* is another symptom of scientific management in education today. Academic units generally have specific requirements about particular faculty actions—post your office hours outside your office, submit grades to the registrar no later than a week after finals, and so on—but it is a bad sign if detailed best practices about pedagogy (or even research) are created and distributed to faculty. These are covert attempts (perhaps entirely unconsciously) to deskill the faculty, to set up systems of education into which any warm body can be inserted in the role of professor, no matter how little knowledge, experience, or insight they have.

Only one of Taylor's principles seems at first to be a bit of an awkward fit in modern higher education: principle (4) on piece-rate pay. But actually, this principle is the germ of the mania for educational assessment. In Taylor's time, it was easy to measure the conformity of workers to the precise timing and motions they were instructed to follow: such actions would result in a certain number of widgets produced. In education, some similarly crude numerical measures can be used—the number of students who are given the grades "D", "F", or "W" is often announced with great importance in faculty performance reviews on our campus—but even though something must be done to evaluate in a black-and-white manner professors' performance, it is said that they cannot simply be left to judge the effectiveness of their teaching or research (deskilled and infantilized as they are).

The centrality of deskilling in Taylorism was clear both to Taylor and his opponents. In his *The Principles of Scientific Management* (Taylor 1914), Taylor noted that:

> The ingenuity and experience of each generation – of each decade, even, have without doubt handed over better methods to the next. This mass of rule-of-thumb or traditional knowledge may be said to be the principal asset or possession of every tradesman.

Then he described the benefit of his approach:

> The managers assume, for instance, the burden of gathering together all of the traditional knowledge which in the past has been possessed by the work-men and then of classifying, tabulating, and reducing this knowledge to rules, laws, and formulæ which are immensely helpful to the workmen in doing their daily work.

But what about in creative industries where the whole point is the innovative, irreducibly original work the workers do? Or what about an industry where the autonomy and agency of the workers is an essential ingredient of their labor? For example, higher education is a creative industry in this sense (in the scholarship-generating aspect of the university) and also one in which worker autonomy cannot be abandoned (since faculty cannot teach autonomy and agency without having some measure of it themselves, as we have noted before). In fact, the very idea of academic freedom—not coincidentally articulated by the American Association of University Professors in the year after Taylor published his *Principles*—is designed exactly to preserve the autonomous creativity which universities require. Academic freedom is the specific line in the sand drawn to prevent the destructive invasion of academia by Taylorism.

During his lifetime, Taylor's scientific management and its necessary ingredient of deskilling drew the criticism that it was dehumanizing workers. "We are not mere machines; we are human beings, and protest against being discussed and con-sidered as coequal with machinery," wrote one critic in 1911 (Duncan 1911). Of course, Taylor didn't want the human workers to become, physically, machines. He only wanted to control their movements precisely; to give them detailed instruction to follow rather than to let them think for themselves. To use a term that was coined only five years after Taylor's death (by Karel Čapek in his play *Rossum's Universal Robots*), scientific management needs to turn workers into robots. Using instead more modern, Internet Age terminology, we could say that Taylorism's goal is for the managers to write and install a program on those robots. This program leaves the workers little choice, free will, or opportunities to exercise their own judgement—just like an *app*, rather than a *program*, it respects the wishes of manage-ment and not the user. The connection with our over-arching metaphor for educa-tion should be clear.

Learning Management Systems

Now let's consider educational Taylorism in action. A learning management system (LMS) is a software suite which is designed to encompass all, or nearly all, of the IT functions required for pedagogy in a modern university. These usually include a gradebook, scheduling tools, and hosting for class materials (handouts, video, audio, images, data—anything that can be on a computer), and sometimes have submission portals for assignments, automated homework and even quizzes or tests, discussion groups and wikis, virtual classrooms, and so on. LMSs are often integrated with the campus authentication architecture so that students and faculty can use their school accounts to login and access or modify their private information, turn in or hand back assignments, do quizzes, and so on.[3] Commercial (nonfree) LMSs include Blackboard, Desire2Learn, Schoology, and many others, while FLOSS LMSs include Canvas, Moodle, Sakai, and others; the FLOSS LMSs can usually be used through a commercial hosting and service company, while the commercial LMSs often have many different service levels including some with local hosting and minimal support and others hosted on the company's servers and strongly supported.

The problems with using LMSs are manifold. The first is based on the closed software and data ecosystem an LMS creates; this can be a strength in that everything within the LMS is designed to interoperate smoothly. But far more than being a strength, this closed system is a terrible flaw. The warm and comfortable environment of the LMS is actually surrounded by a high wall that prevents students from showing or using (or even preserving for the future) their class work and faculty from easily bringing in resources and tools from the wild, open Internet and integrating them into the learning environment. In particular, nothing unexpected or unplanned—innovative—can be brought in, and nothing wonderful can be shared outward or preserved after the end of the semester.

There's actually a very strong parallel here with recent world events: Edward Snowden, a former contractor for the U.S. National Security Agency (NSA), leaked a vast trove of information in 2012 about the NSA's surveillance of the global Internet. Leaked documents made it clear that the NSA had worked with American companies such as AT&T, Google, Microsoft, Verizon, and Yahoo to install intercept devices and software which allowed most catholic data-gathering capabilities—the internal motto was apparently "collect it all" (Greewald 2013). The reaction was swift, particularly outside the United States, condemning this surveillance and calling for ways to prevent it in the future. One of the ideas discussed widely (Brown (2013), Meinrath (2013), and many others) was a move to split the Internet into more pieces with local control, termed *Balkanization of the Internet*, preventing the United States, and the NSA in particular, from having as much control in the future.

Internet Balkanization would be a disaster in so many ways. Current isolated national subnets, like the Internet in China which is heavily controlled and censored and which sits behind a great barrier known as the Great Firewall of China, can be used as instruments of repression and control. The greatest powers of the Internet are its openness and global reach: a great deal of sociological research on innovation (e.g. Burt 2004) describes which (social) network structures foster the creation of new ideas, and all agree that the network must at least be connected. Balkanization allows repression and depresses innovation. LMSs seek to partition the Internet and to keep the pedagogical activities on one campus isolated from the open Internet. That's a bad thing for teaching, scholarship, and especially the scholarship of teaching. Lessons learned on one campus stay on that campus and professors elsewhere make the same mistakes again.

Another issue with LMSs is the structure of resources and services for a course within the LMS, often referred to, in this context, as the *layout of the course*. Often, this structure is quite constrained by the LMS's software. In fact, many universities offer templates for courses that constrain course layout even more, by institutionalizing the perceived best practices in the code itself.[4] The danger to academic freedom here is specific, constraining, and dangerous.

Worse yet, those templates, or even just the layout tools and choice available to LMS users frequently change. It seems like all commercial LMS vendors upgrade their software and change interfaces, layouts, tools, add-ons, and so on, every couple of years. There is nothing wrong with changing, hopefully for the better, a user interface in a piece of software, but the problem with the LMS upgrade cycle is that it is not motivated by the needs of the professors and students. If a vendor came into university classrooms every few years and took away all of the students' ring binders to replace them with spiral-bound notebooks, and then, later, to take away pens and replace them with mechanical pencils, or some such arbitrary change, everyone would be furious. Yet somehow something more invasive with an LMS upgrade is taken merely with a sigh.

Next, when students work outside an LMS, but using all the exciting new Internet-enabled technologies (remember, we are not anti-technology at all) they learn valuable skills and frequently end up with skills and specific work products that will be very valuable to them in the future. Most professionals (certainly faculty) reuse parts of earlier work—maybe a nicely formatted web page, some useful bibliography entries that they often rely on, or a well-explained point on a discussion forum. It makes no sense that such materials are locked in a proprietary format inside the LMS, blocking their reuse.

The legal complexities with the use of LMSs are yet another reason for faculty not to use them. Certainly, the information that users post on an LMS course site must follow all applicable copyright laws, subject also to different considerations if the material is open to the whole Internet or for students enrolled in the particular class and signed in to the LMS. But one might wonder who owns the whole course layout itself, and specific copyrightable (or otherwise ownable) materials loaded onto an LMS site. The good news is that LMS vendors do not seem ever to assert ownership of materials or layouts: this is usually written into contracts those vendors have with their client universities and sometimes explained to the respective campus communities.

The bad news, however, is that whatever are the formalities of legal ownership of, say, a course layout in an LMS, the vendor has possession, that crucial nine-tenths.

We say this because the course site files, even if they are hosted on a university's own servers, are in proprietary formats and only can be accessed with the LMS software itself. So, for example, if a license with the vendor ends, there is no way to get at that course layout, even if the copyright is owned by the university, or more likely, by the instructor who originally created the layout using the LMS's tools and capabilities. Of course, there might be a special contractual provision to handle this kind of situation, but even that means little if the vendor goes out of business, for example.

While we are on the subject of legal problems with data held by an LMS, it is worth thinking about private educational records. The Family Educational Rights and Privacy Act (FERPA) (20 U.S.C. §1232g) is the controlling federal law in the United States with regard to private student academic records, although some state laws also can apply in particular states and situations. This is the law which makes it illegal (not to mention rude and of possible negative pedagogical consequences) to post student grades on a professor's office door, with the actual student names.

Many LMSs advertise as being "FERPA-compliant." Presumably what this means is that they have no obviously FERPA-violating practices, such as exposing all private data on an open website. But whether the actual security protections are state-of-the-art and correctly implemented is anyone's guess: IT security is a tough business, and it is hard to remember to use good security in every place private data is stored, or whenever it is moved or accessed. Furthermore, whether the LMS's user interface makes it easy to protect privacy or to violate it can be quite subtle.

The contract between a university and its LMS vendor should always contain provisions that identify who is responsible for FERPA violations and what the vendor will do to prevent them, although that last is often very vague ("the vendor uses state-of-the-art security technologies but abjures all responsibility in the event of their failure" might be a summary of some of these provisions). Regardless of what the contractual provisions are, it is of course possible that they will not stand up in court. A sufficiently severe breach of private data might lead to suits placing responsibility with either university or LMS vendor, with either side showing negligence, it might be alleged.

It is important to realize that data with legal implications for privacy reasons is necessary in a university IT system, useful to help work with particular students and for curricular improvement, but can be dangerous when retained or used improperly. A good way to think of such data (due to Maciej Cegłowski (Cegłowski 2015)) is as radioactive waste: it is an unavoidable byproduct of the organization's primary purpose but is extremely difficult to get rid of, retaining its danger for a very long time. The standard approach in the IT world, then, called *data minimization*, is to keep the absolute least amount of privacy-relevant data at all times, and to destroy that data as soon as it has served its immediate purpose—no matter the temptation[5] to keep it around forever in case it later becomes useful. Data retention for private data, instead, is an expensive lawsuit waiting to happen.

At the risk of sounding alarmist, or of stubbornly refusing innovations which have enormous positive potential, we are very nervous about the collection of data on students (and, for that matter, faculty). LMSs can, and some do, collect very precise information about student behavior, as do automated homework systems. There is yet much more information linked to individual students in the log files of the campus bookstore, library, dining hall, recreation center, and appointment desks at the counseling, advising, and tutoring centers. On many campuses, students must register their networked devices, which means that metadata saved by the campus routers have a great deal of information about the individual students' online activities. Student emails handled by the campus email system reside on university servers; they could be subject to data mining, just as Google mines the information in Gmail. While some part of this activity is protected by FERPA and its analogue for health information, the Health Insurance Portability and Accountability Act (HIPAA), much is not.

Students today seem to be much more willing to sign away legal privacy protections for better targeted advertising or other incentives (see, e.g., a study *Is online privacy over?* from the USC Annenberg Center for the Digital Future (Annenberg 2013)). So they might be willing to sign a release when they enroll, giving access to all information the university and its IT infrastructure such as the LMS collect, in return for which they would get maybe something like more targeted employment opportunities upon graduation, and, oh, some personalized advertising.

Or else universities could sell to advertisers that portion of the data they collect which is not protected by FERPA and HIPAA, which might also be fairly valuable. FERPA allows universities to release what it calls *directory information* without specific student permission. This information is defined by the educational institutions themselves, within certain parameters, and almost always includes things like name, permanent and local address, residence status, date and place of birth, major and minor fields of study, dates of attendance, degrees and awards received, participation in officially recognized activities and sports, and so on. Some of this has to be very interesting to potential advertisers, and therefore worth something.

We are not saying that collecting and aggregating all possible information on students is inherently inappropriate; if grades, eating habits, gym activity, and so on, can target an intervention that helps a deeply depressed student, we can only praise the effort. But it is getting to the point in the Internet Age that new, highly aggressive data collection regimes have led to problems often enough that we should expect privacy considerations to be equally aggressively defended as simply a matter of good design and policy.

It is worth noting that the great majority of the problems we have just identified with LMSs are largely restricted to the situation of nonfree LMSs, simply because they are not actually under the control of their client universities. An open, FLOSS LMS will not change user interfaces at the LMS provider's whim and against the wishes of the client university—provider and client are the same. Nor can users lose access to their layouts or particular course materials, hidden in the vendor's servers and proprietary data formats: the formats are public (it's FLOSS) and the servers are probably the client's own. FLOSS LMSs also tend to have less of the feeling of an isolated walled garden, since that is contrary to the culture of FLOSS. If a professor wants a module that allows a particular kind of access to an LMS-external resource, it has probably already been written and shared, and if not, someone could always write it.

Of course, commercial LMSs also have a high price-tag, which could be saved by running a FLOSS LMS internally, or going completely without an LMS and simply supporting faculty in putting together whichever tools they feel will best serve their particular course and approach. However, the question usually debated here is what would be the total cost of ownership in each scenario, and the answer is a bit complicated: there are quite different hardware and personnel costs in each, and in the end the decision may actually come down to one's tolerance for risk balanced against one's desire for flexibility and control.

Perhaps the greatest problem with an LMS is when it is imposed on faculty. If some faculty members should want a particular LMS because they think it is the best tool for their pedagogy, based on their (artisanal) experience, knowledge, and insight, then we must respect that (subject to financial and legal care). When an LMS and templates or detailed best practices are imposed on faculty, it is the rankest of Taylorism with all of the problems that entails, particularly in a creative and autonomy-perpetuating industry such as higher education.

The other great problem is waste. It is a waste of money to pay for a commercial LMS. The walled garden of an LMS is a wasted opportunity for unexpected innovation and student learning of tools from the wider web. And the whole complex of features in most modern LMSs is a waste simply because faculty members don't use them. A survey on our campus showed that a large majority of users of our LMS take advantage only of its ability to distribute quite static information (such as reminders and handouts)—which is exactly what the vanilla web is so fantastic at doing—and the online gradebook. We do not know of a secure, stand-alone, online gradebook, but it would be a fairly straightforward task to make one in this day and age. It follows that, given what most users do with their LMSs, we should acknowledge that *An LMS is a heavyweight solution to a lightweight problem*.

A Modest Proposal

The Taylorists in the IT industry impose a strong division of roles between the managers, who observe and then create detailed plans, and the workers, who are thoroughly deskilled and should simply implement the plans in robot-like fashion. In a university, the division between the management and workers is easily visible in an employee's title. The managers are *staff*—sometimes with a little embellishment, such as the *administrative/professional staff* on our campus—and workers are *faculty*.

(From this perspective, the students are the *product*. Thus the trichotomy heard so frequently on a university campus "faculty, staff, and students" can be translated as "workers, managers, and products.")

However, this must be an oversimplification, since there are certainly some workers in a university who are not faculty—secretaries, facilities maintenance personnel, recruiters, sports coaches, electricians, and so on. From this perspective, what distinguishes the faculty from other workers is that they have used their indispensability in the academic project (some form of faculty is a *sine qua non* for a university) to win a bulwark, academic freedom, against excessive Taylorist invasion of their work lives. Until all the janitors on a campus band together and insist upon being granted "janitorial freedom" because a university cannot exist without the waste baskets being emptied, faculty will have a uniquely protected position. (Much of the rest of this book is about how precarious this position is.)

One group of staff on some university campuses has successfully effected a transition to a more protected position like the faculty's—in fact, exactly like faculty. Librarians on many (but certainly not all) universities' campuses in the United States are classified as faculty, with tenure (and non-tenure) lines, positions in the faculty governing bodies (such as faculty senates), expectation of scholarly output, support for attendance at conferences, and so on.

This is not at all a ridiculous status for librarians to have. It would be hard to imagine a university without some form of library, be it one with miles of stacks housing blocks of wood pulp or simply an air-conditioned server room full of electronic resources. Librarians can practice and teach the skill of research, without which a university graduate would seem to be seriously deficient. Librarianship is a rapidly changing discipline and new work in the field is written in peer-reviewed journals and presented at conferences. Finally, the *core values of librarianship,* as expressed by the American Library Association (ALA), include intellectual freedom, the public good, service, and social responsibility, among others (see ALA 2004), which sound a lot like the language from the foundational AAUP documents, starting with (AAUP 1915), creating the term "academic freedom."

Having been brought into the now-larger tent for the faculty, librarians are more able to pursue the above core values, thinking of them as parts of the larger protection of academic freedom. Since this is exactly what protects from the ravages of Taylorist deskilling in a creative industry, librarians as faculty are free to be independent and creative. They can defend, as best their own judgment tells them to do, the goals of the academic project against management which may be distracted by financial, political, or other pressures. This makes them allies of the faculty in preserving the pedagogical and scholarly excellence of their universities.

But note that the ALA's core values also include access and confidentiality/privacy. These values (along with the others mentioned above) are ones which faculty would love to see in the IT professionals on their campuses. So here is our modest proposal: why not make campus IT staff into faculty? Just like in the library, where there are staff who shelf books and perform other support functions and who are not faculty, we suggest that there should be some IT staff who do hardware and network installations and repairs, and other basic support tasks, who are not faculty. But other IT workers who choose and set up complex systems, work with students and faculty for pedagogy and research, have advanced, highly specialized training, and who are expected to research and develop new systems for their universities, **should be faculty**.

With faculty status come the protections of academic freedom, which would allow these IT faculty to speak independently of pressure from management, to work for the right thing from a pedagogical and scholarly IT perspective, rather than simply to follow orders and do what is convenient for control or politics or economics. As one example, in a recent conference with a university IT professional (whom we leave anonymous to protect his job), one of us was told that it would be impossible to use FLOSS software on that campus, because the administration liked the control of having a contract with a commercial (nonfree) software vendor instead. FLOSS software is said to require more, and more qualified, IT staff, but might nevertheless be cheaper than a nonfree approach—and those qualified staff are then available to customize the FLOSS software and to innovate with other members of the university community. However, the culture on this person's campus makes it impossible to go with the cheaper solution of more qualified staff rather than the expensive solution of having a straightforward contractual relationship with a commercial provider.

We should note that the impulse to use external commercial suppliers when a free solution might be possible in-house, or to bring in consulting firms to propose solutions to campus problems, is a strategy which arises from the hegemony of strict Taylorism. Remember that Taylorist management has taken over the role of directing every last movement and rest break, while workers have been deeply deskilled. If a fairly sophisticated product is needed in the organization, it cannot be that it can be designed, built, or operated entirely with existing workers—they've already been deskilled. External organizations can be a source of high-quality products and services, since it is not a necessary tenet of management that those outside their organization are without skills, the way it is necessarily their opinion of their own workers. The same is true of consulting problems brought in to solve a larger problem of organization or strategic planning.

We recognize that this proposal has little chance of getting through university administrations. There is also a very strong external price pressure on skilled IT professionals, since industry pays so much better—this was apparently not a problem for librarians. As a consequence of this price pressure and the lack of the lure of independence and faculty staff, the sad reality is that campus IT departments tend to exhibit a broad mix of talent and knowledge.

Worse than the mere breadth of talent levels, there is the problem that under the current system, and the one which we think will persist, campus IT staff usually have little incentive (or possibility) to be innovative, or to take risks. The best plan for the deskilled Taylorist worker (other than revolution, maybe) is simply to follow orders as much, and as mindlessly, as possible. As a consequence, and giving up hope for freeing the wage slaves in IT departments, it is necessary for faculty to become much more involved in IT strategy, decisions, and even operations, That is the only way that employees with protections and therefore who are motived by the real academic project, will be pushing campus IT in the right decisions.

As one example of this point, faculty need to play a much more assertive and directional role in their campus websites. Many campus IT staff come from industry and not an academic track with advanced degrees and a goal of scholarship, as our modest proposal would have had them be. IT staff with industry experience, or even who simply are trained in and who follow current best practices in web design are going to think of the university website as if it were a commercial site. They will speak often of *search engine optimization (SEO)*, the process of making a site, particularly the pages deep in the site where customers can spend their money, maximally visible to search engines, since this is how most users find products and services on the web. However, students and scholars use a university website for learning and research, not buying widgets.

Automated Homework Systems

So Taylor would have faculty deskilled and almost turned into robots. The most robot-like version of a faculty function would be if it were actually performed by a robot, or computer program. This is actually happening for thousands of math students in universities across the United States, at least in one aspect of their education: grading of homework. Most universities which go this route use software provided by the publisher of their mathematics textbooks, which in fact comes bundled with the book. Pearson sells *MyMathLab*, for example, while McGraw Hill has *ALEKS*.

These automated homework grading systems used to come in the form of a CD-ROM from which the student would install the software on their personal computer. Instead, now they are almost all entirely web-based, so the students access their homework assignments in a web browser. This has the advantage of enormous resources being available on the provider's servers, such as video clips explaining techniques which the student can click on if stuck. In addition, detailed information about the student's progress and grades are instantly available in the instructor's gradebook. However, web-based versions do require the student always to work at a computer that is on the Internet. Most universities do not consider this a problem, because evidence suggests fewer and fewer students, even economically disadvantaged students, lack broadband Internet connections; or even if they do, campuses have computer labs where the students can work on their homework.

Publishers advertise these systems as being superior to the old-fashioned way of grading because the feedback is instant. You would not teach a young person to hit a baseball by having them swing and then waiting 24 hours until telling them if they hit the ball at all, the analogy goes, so why delay homework grades? Further, instructors may (although rarely do, it is claimed) put only a few pointed comments on an incorrect solution. The program, instead, can precompute a huge number of incorrect solutions and recognize what each one indicates about where the student is failing to understand something. Then the program can, if desired by the student or instructor (and if the system allows it, which not all do), require the student to take a time out from the current homework set and refresh some prior material that is apparently not sufficiently mastered.

Finally, the advertisements for these systems point out all of the interactive instructional tools available instantly to the student who is stuck. Typical ad copy (this for students who will use ALEKS) says:

> ALEKS interacts with you much as a skilled human tutor would, moving between explanation and practice as needed, correcting and analyzing errors, defining terms and changing topics on request. By accurately assessing your knowledge, ALEKS focus clearly on what you are ready to learn next, helping you master the course content more quickly and easily.
>
> *(ALEKS 2016)*

So there is no need to wait until the course instructor's office hours, there will be animations of worked examples, videos of short lectures, and readings on just the right techniques—all learning styles accommodated.

When it comes to all the problems with these systems, the devil is in the details. For example, the system absolutely must recognize all expressions which are equivalent to the one it was expecting. This is only a software engineering problem, it is true, but it is surprisingly hard to get right. Another thing that is quite hard is building a system that is very easy to use. For example, most students do not learn a standard way of entering complex mathematical expressions into an input cell on a web page. The most common approach the programs use is to have a panel of tiles which each do a particular piece of algebra notation, so the student mouses around at great length, clicking, then typing numbers and symbols, clicking some more, and so on. Finally, setting up the parameters of the additional help features correctly requires good judgment. Some systems have a *show me a similar example* button, but the students quickly figure out that by pressing this button repeatedly, they will eventually be shown essentially the exact problem they must do for credit. So it is tempting to turn off this feature entirely, but then the interactive help is lost.

The second problem with these automated systems is that all of the advertisements about features completely miss the true reasoning behind the decision to use these systems. It is not the instant feedback or the mastery learning approach or any such high-minded purpose, instead it is simply to patch over an awkward economic reality. These systems used around the United States are mostly for the quite basic courses, from statistics (a service course for nursing students, often) and college algebra (which is the content that used to be taught in high school algebra courses) down to remedial classes on basic algebraic manipulation and even arithmetic. Such courses are overwhelmingly taught by adjuncts. The adjuncts are paid starvation wages[6] and so must teach five or more sections in order to put together a living wage. These classes are usually full, so five sections amounts to a huge number of students. So there is just no way the adjunct instructors can keep up with grading so many students.

Automated homework systems (in mathematics, at least) are a small bandage put over the perhaps mortal wound which is the collapse of public funding for higher education and the rise of the all-adjunct university. If, as a society, we actually wanted to educate students, to keep America from falling too far behind in math and sciences, we would increase funding and help every student to have real interactions with a live human instructor. Automated grading instead is a merely cosmetic solution.

The last problem with these automated homework systems starts to appear when you look at which courses use them. These are quite basic mathematics courses, and sometimes courses in physical science. Essentially, they are courses where the goal seems to be to teach the students to follow a mindless algorithm and to get the right answer, to *program them*. In fact, there are computer programs which can do most of the exercises in such classes—which begs the question, Why are we teaching our students to do merely something that a machine can do? Why wouldn't we just let the machine do it?

These classes, which are often called (appallingly without irony or despair) *drill-and-kill classes,* would be instantly recognizable to anyone who came through the American K-20 educational system. Problem solutions in these classes which are highly praised consist of a page of scribbled symbols and numbers entirely without words, and

$$x = <\text{some number}>$$

at the bottom of the page.

This is not mathematics, nor is it an education worth the name. It is what passes for mathematics education, but the function it serves best is training factory workers or soldiers. Someone who can survive this soul-deadening approach to mathematics is ready to be a Taylorist worker. Automated homework systems for such drill-and-kill classes are machines being used to turn young humans into obedient flesh machines themselves. To those of us who got out of the drill-and-kill torture by accident or luck and who therefore learned the beauty and power of mathematics, who were encouraged to follow curiosity and develop creativity (rather than rote algorithm-following), math education of this form is a painful travesty—Paul Lockhart's *A Mathematican's Lament* (Lockhart 2009) and the essays from the section **Unschool** in Aaron Swartz's *The Boy Who Could Change the World: The Writings of Aaron Swartz* (Swartz 2016) sing this dirge.

Putting aside the failures of mathematics education, what about automated grading in other disciplines? While programs that grade essays are starting to appear, they seem quite primitive so far. As such, they provide even less valuable educational insight than such systems in mathematics, so they distract observers from the real economic goal (of enabling the all-adjunct university) even less. In addition, they are fairly easy to trick, since they assess mostly small-scale syntactic rule-following and some over-all structural features. But meaningful written work mixes syntax and semantics at a fundamental level—think of Chomsky's famous syntactically correct nonsense sentence "Colorless green ideas sleep furiously" (Chomsky 2002)—so a purely syntactic evaluator, as a computer program must be, will never even be able to separate nonsense from good sense, no less meaningfully evaluate complex written work.

Building semantic understanding from programmed manipulation only of syntax is a long-held goal of the entire field of artificial intelligence. Consider the famous *Turing test*, proposed by Alan Turing in 1950 as a way of telling if a machine were truly "intelligent" (Turing 1950). In this thought experiment, Turing imagined that a human would be connected to another entity by merely typing words into a computer, in some natural human language, and reading replies on the screen, asking questions and discussing matters of mutual interest. If, after some period of such conversation, the human could not tell if the correspondent was another human or was a computer, then the computer would be said to be intelligent.

Now consider a university course with small writing assignments at every class meeting. Imagine that the instructor, obviously a human, takes the students' writings away after each class, and returns them at the next class with comments responding to the students. Such communications constitute a Turing test being performed to determine if the grading entity is a computer or is the human instructor working outside class. One side of exactly the dialog which one might use in a more formal Turing test could be the contents of a student's writings each time, and the responses would have to be the grading entity's human-simulating responses in order for them to make sense as comments on that writing.

What this means is that true, high-quality grading of student written work requires another human, or a program implementing, in the formal sense of a Turing test, a human-level artificial intelligence. So the next time someone says they have a really useful essay-grading program, the appropriate response is to praise them for their imminent receipt of the Turing Award (the equivalent of the Nobel Prize in computer science) for having created human-level AI.

Notes

1 This is a paraphrase. For more, see (Taylor 1914).
2 Even though this book is concerned with higher education, we should mention that much of this discussion of scientific management, and particularly principle (4) as assessment, applies in exactly the same way to K-12 education. The simplest, most mechanical (and least useful) educational assessment is standardized testing. The disastrous consequences of the U.S. federal law known as *No Child Left Behind* and its successor *Race to the Top* are in some large part the result of standardized testing, see (Au 2011).
3 The best such are *single sign-on*, where the users login once on their desktop, laptop, or mobile device, and then are seamlessly authorized to use all appropriate resources and services without having to login again to each.
4 Well, actually, it is in the configuration files of the LMS, not its code; anyway, in the software.
5 Apparently the same temptation the NSA feels all the time.
6 On our campus, an adjunct was hired who was not a U.S. citizen and so needed to be sponsored for a work permit—but the pay he was getting was so low that the Immigration and Naturalization Service (INS) did not consider him employed full-time and would not give him the permit.

7

SOCIAL MEDIA IN THE CLASSROOM AND OUT

Going Viral

In 2009, Monica Rankin, Professor of History at the University of Texas at Dallas, began experimenting with Twitter in her classroom. Her goal was to pull more of her ninety students into the class conversation by projecting tweeted questions onto the screen and then answering them. That way, students didn't have to talk to so many people at once and therefore the conversation might be more inclusive. The class also had a teaching assistant who could then send the students direct messages, in order to follow up on their points and questions. Students could even use their tweets as study notes (Smith 2009).

Some people might scoff at the idea of having an intellectual discussion with Twitter's famous 140-character limit, but Rankin instructed her students to post more than one tweet if necessary. Rankin considered her experiment a success because of the way that it opened up the discussion to more students, but in notes posted after the end of the class she noted that,

> the 'discussions' were more constructive if I circulated around the room and made myself available for comments, questions, and other direct feedback. By circulating around the room, I could respond directly to students and I could get suggestions from them of other topics they wanted to address.

In other words, this particular social media experiment depended upon her presence and input in order to work. Indeed, she also noted that students hardly tweeted about the class at all when they were not present in the classroom (Rankin 2009).

The value of social media in this experiment was to counteract the difficult pedagogical situation she faced with a ninety-person classroom. That's why a video about Rankin's experiment quickly went viral, meaning it was viewed by many thousands of interested people. Certainly, making huge classes seem smaller is really admirable. Rankin could have just kept lecturing and let her students sink or swim. At least this way, she and her teaching assistants can give students the kind of direct contact between students and teachers that MOOC enrollees sorely lack. But on the other hand, what if Twitter becomes an excuse for UT-Dallas administrators to make introductory history classes even bigger? Ninety students isn't all that many in the great scheme of things. Once you show management that you can handle the chocolate wrapping line at a reasonable velocity, they're going to speed it up even more. Unfortunately, most of us are too dedicated to offer extra students a substandard education if we consider that part of our jobs. When the people on the line are forced to work harder for the same pay, quality goes down.

Commercial digital tools can also be hard to control. If you aren't paying for the free service that you're using, it's likely that the format that you are used to will eventually change whether you want it to or not. This is not only true of Twitter (which recently replaced starred favorites with hearts for likes, much to the disgust of many academic users), but of other free services like blog-hosting sites. Of course, the same can be said of learning management systems. Perhaps the only way to prevent this from happening is for you to learn to code, something few academics are willing to do.

What social media tools like Twitter or Facebook offer that no LMS can is the ability to reach a potentially limitless number of people in the world outside of academia. While Rankin's experiment was designed to take place entirely within the confines of the classroom, other professors have used Twitter or Facebook to reach out to people in the wider world—much like the connectivist cMOOCs of Canadian origin discussed in Chapter 3. Deliberately or even accidentally, social media can bring the authors of books which a class might be discussing into that discussion, or experts on any particular field with a different view from the professor's. This kind of teaching in public is impossible in a traditional classroom setting, but then again what's said in a traditional classroom setting is unlikely to bring in the kind of unwelcome scrutiny that some professors on social media have already encountered.

Before recounting some well- and lesser-known social media horror stories which also went viral, it is worth first considering the dog that didn't bark. Outside of academia, it has become commonplace for employers to check Facebook and Twitter accounts of potential hires (Davidson 2014). To imagine that this isn't happening in academia—even with its supposed free speech protections—is simply naive. Nobody can know what interviews they didn't get because of their social media postings. More importantly, the way academic employment works, people off the job market will never know what additional opportunities they might have gotten if it were not for their social media activities. Still, plenty of professors post controversial statements on social media without necessarily realizing the risk that they're taking by doing so.

In more than a few cases, professors who took this chance paid a steep price. For example, on September 16, 2013, University of Kansas (KU) Journalism Professor

David Guth condemned the National Rifle Association (NRA) in a tweet on his personal Twitter account after a shooting incident at the Washington Naval Yard in Washington, D.C. KU initially defended Guth's right to post the tweet even as it separated itself from its content, but following a week of pressure from the public and two state legislators, the University of Kansas suspended him (Foundation for Individual Rights in Education 2014). Later that year, the Board of Regents that oversees the Kansas university system instituted a new policy regarding the "improper use of social media." They revised the policy after criticism that "some portions of the policy could lead to professors being fired simply for disagreeing with university policies or their colleagues online" but it remains extraordinarily restrictive, allowing professors to be terminated for postings that fall within their rights under the First Amendment to the United States Constitution (Summers 2014).

Steve Salaita is a world-renowned scholar of indigenous studies who was going to leave the English Department at Virginia Tech for the Native American Studies Department at the University of Illinois Urbana Champaign (UIUC). Salaita posted a series of controversial tweets about Israel and Palestine after receiving a job offer but before that offer was approved by UIUC's Board of Trustees. At first, the University defended Salaita's right to tweet such things, even as they distanced the university from his ideas. But this tolerant position didn't last. Chancellor Phyliss Wise changed her mind about the Salaita appointment and never sent it for approval by the Board (Palumbo-Liu 2014). Salaita sued, and in late 2015 the two sides reached a large financial settlement (Palumbo-Liu 2015).

The difference between these disputes is that Guth kept his job and Salaita didn't, but their similarities are more disturbing. They demonstrate an increased tendency of university administrators to bend to pressure regarding academic freedom, even on issues that are directly relevant to a professor's work—like with Salaita's criticism of Israel. In both cases, the reason outside interests found the tweets that caused these professors trouble was their presence on social media, which expands the reach of anyone's particular ideas to countless friends and foes alike.

While we tend to think of going viral as something exclusively for cat videos or ice bucket challenges, the same thing can happen to professors like Guth or Salaita precisely because there is a large segment of the American population that doesn't like professors and wants to embarrass all of us as a class. "Online," writes the Internet analyst Clay Shirky, "the default mode for many forms of communications is instant, global, and nearly permanent. In this world the private register suffers" (Shirky 2008). Whisper something controversial to the professor in the next office over from you and nobody will care. Broadcast it to the world and people who might not like what you have to say may hear you.

What's different about social media from just about any other kind of communication is that more people than just you can decide what gets broadcast to the world. The more friends or followers you have, the more the opinions that you thought were essentially private become public. Professors who were used to toiling in obscurity can become public figures against their will, precisely because social media allows their utterances to reach the class of donors upon which universities beset by austerity now depend, or state legislators who want to cut their budgets even more. While invoking academic freedom makes logical sense, academic freedom has never been tested as readily as it has been in recent years by the sudden fame that social media can willingly or unwillingly bestow upon faculty.

It is important to note that both race and gender can play an important part in exactly how dangerous social media can be to one's career. To be outspoken is risky, but being a woman, or an African–American can attract trolls—angry anonymous people who follow your postings in the hopes that they can use them to derail your career. Saida Grundy, for example, was an incoming Professor of Sociology at Boston University (BU) in the spring of 2015 when she tweeted her opinion about the relationship between white men, race and slavery. Her tweets offended one conservative student with an online publication enough that his outrage attracted the attention of other conservatives who called for Dr. Grundy's ouster. She offered a carefully-worded apology and is still employed by BU (Hetter 2015).

Grundy and Salaita were attacked for tweeting about topics that fall directly within their areas of academic expertise. Guth presumably has no particular insight into gun issues as a journalism professor, much like History Professor Erik Loomis who attracted unwelcome attention for tweeting about the NRA in 2012 (and also kept his job) (Pavlich 2012). The important question that any professor who is politically active on social media has to ask themselves is, "How long will professors who tweet on controversial topics be able to keep their jobs?" Kansas' new social media policy (even after revision) still includes a clause that makes it possible to fire a faculty member for making statements "contrary to the best interests of the employer" (Summers 2014). Steve Salaita received a large settlement from UIUC but as of this writing does not have a permanent job.

Extramural Utterances

What kind of speech by faculty deserves protection? The American Association of University Professors (AAUP) considers two different types of speech when examining the impact of speech restrictions on academic freedom: intramural utterances and extramural utterances. The first is the kind of speech that directly affects your research or your job, like what you say in the classroom. The second is the kind of speech a professor might exercise in their role as a citizen, like letters to the editor or how you might testify at a city council meeting (Eron 2015, 1–2). The AAUP believes that faculty members have a right to exercise both kinds of speech. Many of its earliest efforts to protect academic freedom came from cases where individual professors were fired for making utterances related to their academic expertise (Wilson 2015).

What social media does is to blur the distinction between extramural and intramural utterances. On the one hand, social media isn't really formal publishing. It's primarily for your Twitter followers or your Facebook friends. However, these informal, often off-the-cuff utterances also have the possibility of being broadcast to the world. What makes the Internet so extraordinary, the ability to reach hundreds if not thousands of new readers, is also what makes it so dangerous. Even if surrounded entirely by your Facebook "friends," faculty members have to assume that they are writing in public.

Because controversial viewpoints like Salaita's or Guth's or Grundy's have gone viral, the distinction between intramural and extramural utterances has become increasingly irrelevant. From the administrative point of view, the problem is not whether the professor in question had any special knowledge of the topic, but the fact that their opinions on social media somehow gained large audiences. Don Eron, writing in AAUP's *Journal of Academic Freedom*, argues that the fact that Salaita was an expert in such matters actually made it more likely that he would get attacked for his views. "[B]ecause his comments were in an area of his academic expertise – the situation of Palestinians," Eron writes, "[Salaita] was speaking as an authority. Otherwise, no one would care about his viewpoint" (Eron 2015, 4). While that might be true, it is certainly true that if he didn't post those views on social media nobody would know about his viewpoint. The fact that Salaita was a professor is why enemies of his viewpoint singled him out for harassment among all the people who hold pro-Palestinian views.

As long as we relegate our opinions to little-read journal articles (one study suggests that 50 percent of academic journal articles have only three readers: their author, their editor and an outside commentator), nobody cares about what the faculty think (Eveleth 2014). Writing in the open is the greatest challenge to academic freedom in the Internet Age. People who feel that university professors are biased, or should teach more, will read in our Facebook posts and tweets all the evidence they need to justify making our already austere university budgets more austere still. Of course this is unjust and not conducive to academic freedom, but then again academic freedom has always been something that faculty members have had to fight for in order to preserve.

Ironically, the same media platforms that can get faculty into trouble are also excellent platforms for organizing a fight on behalf of faculty in higher education. Facebook, besides being a place to connect with your friends and family, is a good place for like-minded people to come together in support of their ideas. Twitter, which has millions of users around the world, not only connects those users in an online form of "Six Degrees of Separation," but can unite like-minded users around a single hashtag (an issue or subject preceded with the symbol "#") in a matter of minutes. As long as there are far more faculty than administrators and donors in the world, it seems a safe bet that social media will be populated with far more friends than enemies of particular faculty-related causes.

This is particularly true when your cause is yourself. Imagine a situation in which a department chair, dean or even Provost or President has taken a particular dislike to an individual faculty member. In ordinary situations, if they bend the rules in order to make you suffer, you might have to suffer these indignities alone. On the other hand, sunlight can be a particularly good disinfectant—a means to shame those abusing their power. Universities, like so many other large bureaucratic institutions, seldom enjoy bad publicity. Not just the press in general, but the higher education press in particular often gets its stories from items it first noticed on social media. Therefore, going public in this way can really ensure that a story continues for a long time.

Even when no cause is at stake, social media can be an excellent space for faculty to exchange academic information. Academic Twitter, for example, is a robust sub-section of the larger Twitter community where faculty and graduate students exchange ideas, links and suggestions related to research, teaching, and academic life in general. One of the best features of academic Twitter is the way that it brings people together across disciplines. It also brings together faculty with similar inter-ests across international borders. Yes, it is hard to have a nuanced discussion when you are restricted to 140 characters, but Twitter is often a meeting place for future communications, collaborations and even entire conferences.

Those scholars who study social media closely have begun to see it as a means for improving scholarship of all kinds. For example, the Canadian academic Bon Stewart, who carefully studied the habits of ten highly-networked scholars as part of her dissertation, found that,

> A majority of participants reported that this circulation of ideas and resources not only helped them build new knowledge and become aware of new lit-erature in their fields, but also broadened their understanding of alternate viewpoints in their areas of expertise. Twitter was a site of learning and public scholarly contribution.
>
> *(Stewart 2015)*

To forgo the possibilities of this kind of resource because of fear of political retribu-tion would be a tragedy of the highest order.

Other academic social media places have sprung up as a way to limit the expo-sure of controversial opinions to hostile audiences. Profology (http://profology.com), for example, advertises itself as "the exclusive community for higher educa-tion professionals." To join, you have to "provide verifiable proof that you work or have worked in higher education." Once you're a member you can do all the important professionally-oriented things that people do on sites like LinkedIn or Facebook, "like connect and commiserate with peers." However, on Profology, you don't have to worry that conservative watchdogs are following you because the site isn't open to people other than professors.

On the other hand, any social media site populated entirely by academics cannot offer the same reach as its broader commercial competitors like Twitter because there aren't enough academics who conduct their social media activities solely in their roles as academics. Social media fosters connecting, and persistent complaining and sounding off about all things, not just academic matters, which by definition makes any solely academic version of Facebook or Twitter inherently less interest-ing. Academics alone simply cannot provide the same critical mass that can make something go viral. That's why when something like that happens to any academic (be it because of their statements or their research), the attention is usually hostile.

What makes this tension between impact and unwelcome attention particularly troublesome is that it plays out in environments that individual users cannot control. In fact, having political views that are generally to the left of center, academics are likely to have much greater concerns than the average person with the corporate nature of any social media site, whether it's explicitly designed for them or not. Academia.edu is a commercial site where professors go to post their work and to read other people's research. Unlike expensive for-profit publishers, access to that work is free. The site makes its money by exploiting the data of its users. "We don't have control over what's happening," noted Martin Eve of the Open Library of Humanities in a story about Academia.edu for the *Chronicle of Higher Education* (Wexler 2015). Yet, it is worth noting, that like LMSs or even computer operating systems, users don't have any control over how any commercial, nonfree program they use as part of their academic duties shapes their day-to-day activities.

Whose Social Media Is It?

The root cause of this problem is competition between different interests. Consider LinkedIn, the popular business-oriented networking site. LinkedIn has an interest in getting you to cultivate as many connections as possible because this will encourage you to return as often as possible to LinkedIn. Also, a robust social graph—the network of individuals along with all of their connections, each having some strength—is valuable information which presumably LinkedIn sells to advertisers and others.[1] Apart from the advertising you may click on while there, the more you use LinkedIn, the more likely it is that you'll pay for any of their premium services. Most people interested in employment with conventional businesses probably have no concerns about expanding their personal networks. You never know from where your next job might come. Maybe somebody you barely remember and who barely remembers you will pick you out of their own networks and invite you to apply. Maybe somebody who doesn't know you at all will take an interest in you simply by searching open resumes on LinkedIn as a whole.

However, as any tenured or tenure-track faculty member can tell you, job searching in academia doesn't work in quite the same way as it does elsewhere in the capitalist world. For one thing, academics tend to stay in the same job for much longer than other workers do, especially if they're on tenure-track positions. The most likely step for these folks isn't out, but up into administration and the number of connections that you have outside the university is unlikely to affect those kinds of moves. For academics that really are looking to move elsewhere, those moves are restricted by the narrow specialization associated with most academic jobs. Those who specialize in Russian literature have no concern that there's an opening at a university hospital in their area, but LinkedIn's algorithms often send mismatched notices to academics who register there because their algorithms can't tell the difference.

In our experience, academics using social networks crave social connections less than they do usable information about their fields. Being a particularly good tweeter, for example, is a great way to draw attention to yourself if you happen to be a graduate student or are little known in your field, but plenty of graduate students will lock their Twitter accounts up for job search season over the fear that a hiring committee will search their tweets for incriminating information. However, connecting with people in your exact field over social media can give you information about your job, your research or even your mutual friends from back in graduate school days. Certainly some groups, like adjunct faculty, have transcended these smaller concerns in order to organize as a class, but that kind of activity carries obvious risks. Social media can make faculty in even the most isolated locales feel less intellectually isolated, whether they have thousands of followers and friends or even just a couple of hundred.

What faculty, in particular, must understand is that how they use social media is not always under their control. Of course, this includes the conversations that so many parents have started having with their teenage children these days: Don't drunk-tweet. Don't post a picture of yourself doing anything illegal. Always assume that what you put online is being shared with the whole world because it might very well be. Always check your privacy settings on Facebook, and most importantly, recognize that the interest of any social media site may not align perfectly with your own.

The interests of these private companies depend upon the data you provide them. As the Australian academic Tim Klapdor has explained,

> What's happening is that once you've put your data in then these companies they use this to test and experiment on you. You become part of their universe and domain, a resource they can utilize in a purely cynical and exploitative manner.
>
> *(Klapdor 2015)*

The more connections you have, the more valuable their networks become. It doesn't matter whether those connections are useful or useless to you. It doesn't matter whether those connections are friendly or hostile. Their interest is to assure that everyone is connecting on their platforms so that their platforms become more valuable.

That's why cautious academics need to adopt an extra level of care in these matters because the kinds of conversations that they consider perfectly ordinary or (even worse) protected speech that obviously falls under the canopy of academic freedom might not be able to withstand the scrutiny of hostile audiences not party to these traditions. For example, in 2010, Professor Gloria Gadsden of East Stroudsburg University (ESU) was suspended from her job for posting messages on Facebook that were interpreted as violent threats. At the time, she had only thirty-two friends and "was unsure how her messages wound up at ESU's provost's office." Gadsden blamed her administration's quickness to act against her with respect to this particular incident on an earlier essay that she had written for the *Chronicle of Higher Education* that criticized her school for its failure to retain minority faculty

(Berrett 2010). Whatever the merits of that charge, it nonetheless serves as an important reminder that those faculty who are willing to exercise their free speech rights may not get the same benefit of a doubt that others do when their various social media postings create any kind of confusion.

How should faculty navigate the shifting grounds of social media? We are not telling you to shut up, only to proceed with caution. Lindsay Oden, writing for a graduate student audience, recommends a complete separation of your professional and personal lives on social media. This seems like good advice for everyone in academia. If you want to keep using Facebook (and neither of us do), you can use that site's ever-changing privacy settings to limit which of the people in your networks can see your posts. It is most likely that this would mean keeping your family pictures away from your colleagues, but then you can always show them off around the office if necessary. Along similar lines, Oden also recommends limiting the ability to view your old posts only to friends and making it harder for potential employers just to look you up by changing your privacy settings. Twitter users simply have to get used to the fact that their writings there will always be publicly accessible unless they lock down their account to new followers or communicate exclusively through the direct message function (Oden 2015).

If you happen to be the kind of person who tends towards making strong statements when angry, perhaps you should take Facebook and Twitter off your phone and only use it on your desktop since it's less likely that you'll do something that's potentially career threatening if you have to work to get the program open. If you dislike or are not interested in social media, you could try blogging—a medium that generally requires more deliberation before you post anything. Ironically, despite being on the open Internet, it seems less likely that blog posts will get you in trouble since they don't have the same viral potential as tweets or Facebook postings. Nevertheless, if you (or one of your readers) tweets or Facebooks one of your posts, it then carries the same potential effect as you being on those networks yourself. In other words, these days we are all on social media to some degree whether we want to be or not.

That's why it's so important to make sure that your home institution has some basic protections in place. The sociologist Tressie McMillan Cottom recommends that it has a response prepared should it find itself deluged by angry phone calls or emails. One aspect of that response would be a formal way to receive such a deluge. She also recommends that all universities have a protocol in place for threats against faculty researchers. Explicit protections in your faculty handbook are another good idea. So is being familiar with whatever resources your faculty association or your union has for faculty members who suddenly find they are surprisingly unpopular with the public for whatever reason. To Cottom, these protections are the price for employing public scholars who are told to remain publicly engaged (Cottom 2015).

An even stronger solution to the threats that come with social media use is to help to reconceptualize academic freedom for the Internet Age. A good starting point for this position would be the American Association of University Professors' statement on "Academic Freedom and Electronic Communications" (AAUP

2013a), first issued in 2004 and revised in 2013. The AAUP, of course, has been an important force behind the conception and implementation of academic freedom in America and the world since its founding in 1915. This particular policy statement was intended to help keep that concept in place despite the shifts in power relations that accompany any major shift in the technological landscape. As the statement itself explains, "While basic principles of academic freedom transcend even the most fundamental changes in media, recent developments require a re-examination of the application and implications of such principles in a radically new environment" (AAUP 2013a).

The efforts the AAUP makes along these lines are conservative in the completely non-political sense of that word—meaning that they are intended to conserve the protections that have been established rather than try to create new ones or allow old ones to be rolled back. "Academic freedom, free inquiry, and freedom of expression within the academic community may be limited to no greater extent in electronic format than they are in print," the statement reads. While there might be the occasional "unusual situation" where the "nature of the medium" could give rise to some limitations, the fact is that any extramural faculty utterance is specifically excluded from that formulation later in the statement (AAUP 2013a). In other words, the reach that any electronic communication may have is not an adequate reason to restrict or censor that message.

In the early days of the AAUP, academic freedom was gradually established by taking up the cases of individual professors who had been wronged by their employers. They expressed unpopular beliefs that got them sanctioned or (more likely) fired. Their colleagues organized the Association not just in order to help those who had been victimized, but to help their universities establish policies that would prevent colleagues from being victimized in the future (Tiede 2015). To establish and protect policies that will protect the electronic communications of university professors will require defending people who run afoul of those who want to take academic freedom backwards, even as academia itself goes forwards. Luckily, perhaps the easiest thing to do on social media from a political standpoint is to organize.

An organized faculty can take many forms. Like-minded people come together to discuss topics of mutual interest. Perhaps they start a petition. Perhaps they organize a conference. Perhaps they do nothing but exchange information that informs everyone's world view. From the standpoint of academia, all of these actions can be valuable. However, since academics face the possibility of particular scrutiny for trading in unpopular ideas, at some point it may be best to do some of these things off social media. Published papers are a better place to present challenging ideas than tweets. Books are a better place to explore complex issues than Facebook posts. When you have gotten these ideas out in more traditional fora then by all means use social media to promote them.

Of course, anyone who uses the Internet knows about *trolls*; they are almost always anonymous. As a result, trolls write ugly things that are well outside established professional standards. Trolls who read academic books, review and respond to them under their own name are no longer trolls. They are your critics. Since informed criticism is a part of the normal academic information production process, engaging with your critics is an important means of testing your ideas so that they can have a meaningful impact beyond the ups and downs of the Internet's flavor *du jour*.

Note

1 This is immensely valuable information. For example, Eben Moglen, professor at Columbia University, was told by "a senior government official" that the Justice Department had "come to realize that [it] need[s] a robust social graph of the United States" (Moglen 2012), presumably to find terrorists and other criminals.

8

THE ZERO-MARGINAL-COST EDUCATION

Marginal Costs and Net Neutrality

One of the main reasons the Internet has had such a dramatic impact on so many industries is the marginal cost curve[1] for delivery of units of activity or product that the network brings about. When an individual or geographic area first gets a network connection, the cost of the first few bits is enormous: a neighborhood must have cable (copper or, if you are lucky, the much faster fiber optic) laid for wired connections—the proverbial *last mile*—or cell towers for mobile Internet, and in either case capacity must be increased at the regional and higher levels and the user must buy a computer or smartphone. Once the (enormous) basic price of setting up a fast, nearly universal, and reliable network is recovered, the cost of additional bits plummets to a quite modest number for the consumer.

Actually, that is incorrect: the marginal cost per bit, after the initial installation of infrastructure, is almost infinitesimal—for the Internet Service Provider (ISP). There are two problems. The first is that users want to move around *a lot* of bits. Textual information is quite small: a web version of a course syllabus might be a few dozen kilobytes,[2] likewise an online newspaper article without images, while medium resolution images are again from dozens to a couple hundred KB, and a PDF of a full textbook might be anywhere from most of a megabyte[3] to several MB.

Audio starts to be more data than text. An audio file of an hour-long lecture is often most of 100MB of data. A live audio chat over the Internet, such as using the Skype service, requires about 100 kbps[4] both upstream and downstream, according to the company's FAQ, support.skype.com/en/faq/FA1417/how-much-bandwidth-does-skype-need.

Video is much more bandwidth-intensive: services such as Skype and Google Hangouts suggest around 0.5 to 2.6 mbps[5] both upstream and downstream for a two-party video call, but increasing only for the downstream connection, and only to something in the range 4 to 8 mbps, for a group video conference (see the same Skype FAQ as before, or support.google.com/plus/answer/1216376?hl=en for Google Hangouts).

In terms of the total amount of data, rather than just the bandwidth, note that the video-on-demand provider Netflix advises its users (on the page help.netflix.com/en/node/87) that an hour of video can be in the range 0.5 to 5GB.[6] It's particularly relevant to know what Netflix thinks about this, since Netflix accounts for more than one third of Internet traffic in the evenings in North America (Sandvine 2014).

With such large amounts of data being moved around, even a very modest cost per bit would add up to a fairly substantial total sum. The total expense of providing such a service would also be quite large even if it were very modest per bit. Consider the estimated two-thirds of a million viewers watching all twelve hours of season two of the Netflix series *House of Cards* on the first weekend it was available (Daly 2014), which amounts to approximately 40 PB[7] of data moved around for this one show.

The benefit felt by the consumer of a low marginal cost per bit is thus blunted by the ever-increasing amount of data consumers expect to be able to access. The second problem with the idea that consumers should see great benefit from the nearly infinitesimal marginal cost per bit of a mature network has to do with *net neutrality*.

The United Nations has declared (La Rue 2011) that Internet access is a human right and courts or parliaments in several countries (including Estonia, Finland, France, and Greece) have made specific provisions to realize the goal of universal access. At the same time, in situations where competition for Internet service is very weak, ISPs have an opportunity to use their control of this vital resource to charge different prices for different kinds of data, or for data from different sources. The implicit (sometimes explicit) threat is that the ISP will slow down its delivery of these second-class bits if they are not paid off.

This is particularly a problem in the United States, where a very meager handful of companies control nearly all Internet access, wired or wireless, and the resulting lack of competition has meant that the U.S. has some of the most expensive, lowest quality, and lowest speed Internet in the Global North (see (Crawford 2013) for much more on this story of market failure). Furthermore, since these ISPs have acquired other companies (studios) which produce large quantities of video, or which have large libraries that consumers are anxious to access, the idea of charging different rates or (what amounts to nearly the same thing) changing the speed with which they serve some data streams can be immensely profitable. An ISP can charge more to deliver the data from websites which compete with its own allied data-producing websites, with the effect of raising more money or even of simply putting the competitors out of business. Equal treatment of all digital data, regardless of source, has come to be called net neutrality.

Activists such as the Electronic Frontier Foundation (EFF) have fought very hard for net neutrality, trying to win both general public support and specific court cases. While the prospects for net neutrality seem good at the time of this writing, they are not certain. The Federal Communications Commission (FCC), which has legal jurisdiction over these issues, ruled that the broadband Internet is a "telecom-munications service," reversing a 2002 ruling which held it to be an "information service." This terminology change (technically a "Title II reclassification") has important consequences for the kinds of rules the FCC can impose on ISPs. In particular, the FCC Chairman Tom Wheeler wrote in *WIRED* magazine, about the legal power the FCC would have after reclassification.

> Using this authority, I am submitting to my colleagues the strongest open internet protections ever proposed by the FCC. These enforceable, bright-line rules will ban paid prioritization, and the blocking and throttling of lawful content and services. I propose to fully apply – for the first time ever – those bright-line rules to mobile broadband.
>
> *(Wheeler 2015)*

Obviously, the oligopoly ISPs around the U.S., seeking to protect their chance to use net neutrality violations as a revenue source, have brought cases to prevent Chairman Wheeler's approach from taking hold. At the time of this writing, the outcome is unclear, but we remain optimistic. For more information see the EFF's web pages about net neutrality, starting with eff.org/issues/net-neutrality.

In the world of higher education, new ideas and innovation often come from unexpected directions. Because privileging currently accepted or popular ideas at the expense of alternatives is manifestly anti-academic, net neutrality should be an obvious necessity. The truly free exchange of academic ideas requires the low mar-ginal cost per bit to be shared equally by all bits and not to use demand today for certain bits to increase the cost for the ideas which are starting to appear in other, less well-known bits—otherwise we run the risk of intellectual stagnation. Since traditionally underrepresented groups also (by definition) have poorer representa-tion among the popular and powerful data sources on the Internet, the failure of net neutrality can also serve to institutionalize racial, economic, and other forms of discrimination in the digital world.

Encouraging openness to all ideas requires net neutrality. When closed systems such as nonfree LMSs are used at a university, the additional difficulties (a form of cost) they may impose on getting to particular digital media, or to media from a particular source, threaten the free exchange of ideas. This is then yet another reason that university communities should insist upon free software and open standards.

Works Made for Hire

Let's consider the marginal cost curve in one particular industry specific to educa-tion: textbooks. From the point of view of a textbook author, there is often an initial enormous investment of time (for thinking and writing), hopefully built on a solid foundation of subject-matter expertise (probably acquired during years of schooling and disciplinary practice) as well as pedagogical insight. Some part of that initial investment should be recovered, the author hopes, by the first so many unit sales, after which further sales start to bring in a larger and larger fraction of profit.

Of course, we must also take into account the publisher of this textbook. Employees of the publisher, such as editors and book designers, are often involved, to a greater or lesser extent, in the creation of the book in the first place. After that investment, there are also marketing expenses and the actual costs of manufacturing and distribution, to be borne by the publisher. Contracts with textbook publishers have many related provisions to deal with the financial repercussions of all of these points, including in particular the basic percentage of the profit which the author will receive.

If the author is a professor at a university, one might think that the university itself has a financial interest in this textbook. This is based on a doctrine in copyright law called *works for hire*. Since the basic idea of copyright is to encourage the production of Science and useful Arts, one might think that the ownership of this limited monopoly, the copyright, should be given to the author or artist whom we want to motivate in that production. But sometimes an organization will have employees—long-term or even short-term independent contractors—who do the work on the organization's behalf, and it is considered more important to incentivize the organization to do this work by giving it ownership of any resulting copyrights than it would be to reward the employees personally with this individual right over the collective's product. Products which automatically fall into this category where the organization is given the copyright are called "works made for hire," a term which is defined in the Copyright Act of 1976, 17 U.S. Code §101:

A 'work made for hire' is –

(1) a work prepared by an employee within the scope of his or her employment; or

(2) a work specially ordered or commissioned for use as a contribution to a collective work, as a part of a motion picture or other audiovisual work, as a translation, as a supplementary work, as a compilation, as an instructional text, as a test, as answer material for a test, or as an atlas, if the parties expressly agree in a written instrument signed by them that the work shall be considered a work made for hire. For the purpose of the foregoing sentence, a 'supplementary work' is a work prepared for publication as a secondary adjunct to a work by another author for the purpose of introducing, concluding, illustrating, explaining, revising, commenting upon, or assisting in the use of the other work, such as forewords, afterwords, pictorial illustrations, maps, charts, tables, editorial notes, musical arrangements, answer material for tests, bibliographies, appendixes, and indexes, and an 'instructional text' is a literary, pictorial, or graphic work prepared for publication and with the purpose of use in systematic instructional activities.

It would be perfectly reasonable for universities to assert that all copyrightable products—books, research papers, websites, pedagogical materials, etc.—are in fact works made for hire. Certainly, faculty are employees and such copyrightable products are within the scope of their employment, often entirely explicitly in faculty handbooks, annual evaluations, and work effort calculations subjected to furious negotiations. Point (2) in the legal definition even mentions instructional texts, tests, and so on.

As many faculty can attest, universities seldom assert ownership of copyrights in research articles, books, or instructional materials produced by tenure-line faculty. (With adjuncts, the situation is a little less clear, particularly for instructional materials.) In fact, as faculty authors should already know, when they publish a research article in a journal, they own the copyright at first, but sign it away to the journal as a condition of publication. For a monograph or textbook, instead, faculty members retain the copyright, but the contract with the publisher has very detailed provisions about the distribution of costs and revenues, conditions for re-use or transformative use, and so on.

Why aren't universities attempting to use the idea of works for hire in order to turn the copyrightable products of faculty efforts into additional revenue streams? This question is impossible to answer with certainty, but the answer probably boils down to an historical accident. The tradition was probably set—and, crucially, written into faculty handbooks—in a less neoliberal era, also when it was hard to imagine articles and books would bring in all that much profit.

This tradition continues essentially unchallenged to the present day as part of an unspoken deal that people make when they choose to become university professors. Faculty have skills and a work ethic which would allow them to find good employment fairly easily outside of the academy.[8] Yet universities wish to convince them to take a job with an enormous workload and nevertheless quite low salary. One way to lure them is to offer the abstract satisfaction of feeling they are making a difference in their students' lives and in their chosen academic disciplines. Another is to make it perfectly clear, by not asserting copyright in works for hire, that the products of professors' intellectual labor are entirely their own, to profit from if desired and possible, to sign away copyrights for, if that is necessary for a good publication and the resulting respect of their peers, or even just in a moral sense.

The idea that there could be a "written instrument signed by [the parties] that the work shall be considered a work made for hire" is broached in part (2) of the definition from 17 U.S. Code §101. This underlines the fact that in cases where there could be any ambiguity regarding the status of a professor's copyrightable work as work for hire or not, it is very important to have a prior written document clarifying that status. Usually, this is in a university's faculty handbook, but faculty must check the language for completeness and clarity. Particularly in situations with new technology, policy changes can happen quickly, quietly, and in ways that are not really understood even by those implementing them. For example, on our campus, the faculty handbook has the traditional provisions about copyrightable products of faculty labor. Nevertheless, a change to the acceptable use policy (AUP) for IT resources included the clause "the University retains all ownership rights to all its collective data," which collective data seemed to include all digital files created or even simply stored on a device controlled by the university. A reasonable question then was whether the university would assert ownership in, for example, an essay that a faculty member wrote on their office computer—and our president told the faculty senate it would. Given the direct contradiction with longstanding tradition and specific provisions in our faculty handbook, which of course give faculty the copyrights of their essays, it is unlikely that the president's comment was anything other than misinformed. But this example shows that faculty must remain vigilant if they are to protect their side of the deal they make when taking university employment.

In areas where there is very rapid development and change, tradition may not have had time to catch up. For example, only fairly recently have university professors produced materials which are patentable and have the chance of earning a substantial income (although the actual situation is quite complicated, as we noted in Chapter 4). This explains why patents are treated differently from copyrights, so that universities typically do assert rights over faculty inventions and have specific policies regarding profit sharing. It also explains how very new pedagogical instruments—programs, websites, tools and methodologies of online education, the products of unbundling a course, and so on—are sometimes subject to different rules from older faculty products. Administrations do sometime try to assert control, as the case of Jennifer Ebbeler at the University of Texas at Austin (mentioned above in Chapter 2) suggests.

Open Access for Scholarly Works

The economics of scholarly journal articles have actually received quite a bit of attention, at least in the academic community.[9] In summary, the prices of subscriptions to respected journals have been increasing at spectacular rates, often by several hundred percent over a recent ten-year period (Edwards and Shulenburger 2003). In addition, the costs of producing journals seem quite modest, in part since peer review, the most skill-intensive step, is something scholars do for free as members in the academic community. Also, typesetting is getting easier and easier because of technological improvements. For example, in many scientific fields (certainly including physics, mathematics, and computer science), it is expected that scholars will submit articles to journals in an essentially camera-ready form (usually produced by the FLOSS tool TeX). Finally, today journals are often distributed and read, and certainly searched, electronically, where the low marginal cost per bit is important (and note that scholarly articles are not large chunks of data). "So there are powerful reasons for believing that high and rising prices are due not to costs, but rather to the combination of highly inelastic demand and suppliers' substantial market power" (Edwards and Shulenburger 2003).

The inelasticity of demand is largely cultural, and seems to be beginning to change. New journals and new (electronic) methods of production and distribution are starting to become more popular. Even twenty years ago, the mathematician Andrew Odlyzko, then of Bell Labs, wrote an article (Odlyzko 1995) whose title,

Tragic loss or good riddance? The impending demise of traditional scholarly journals, made his prediction quite clear. He likened the inflexible attitudes then of journal publishers to the similarly inflexible approach that the *Encyclopedia Britannica* had taken to the advent of the Information Age: *Britannica* was completely destroyed by the Internet and, in particular, by the crowd-sourced and FLOSSy Wikipedia.

One exciting change that has happened in these twenty years since Odlyzko predicted the demise of traditional scholarly journals was the increase in acceptance and ease of use of the *open access (OA)* model of scholarly publications.

Peter Suber, a very important philosopher and activist of open access, describes it in his *A Very Brief Introduction to Open Access* (Suber 2004), which reads, almost in its entirety:

> Open-access (OA) literature is digital, online, free of charge, and free of most copyright and licensing restrictions. What makes it possible is the internet and the consent of the author or copyright-holder.
>
> In most fields, scholarly journals do not pay authors, who can therefore consent to OA without losing revenue. In this respect scholars and scientists are very differently situated from most musicians and movie-makers, and controversies about OA to music and movies do not carry over to research literature.
>
> OA is entirely compatible with peer review, and all the major OA initiatives for scientific and scholarly literature insist on its importance. Just as authors of journal articles donate their labor, so do most journal editors and referees participating in peer review.
>
> OA literature is not free to produce, even if it is less expensive to produce than conventionally published literature. The question is not whether scholarly literature can be made costless, but whether there are better ways to pay the bills than by charging readers and creating access barriers. Business models for paying the bills depend on how OA is delivered.
>
> There are two primary vehicles for delivering OA to research articles: OA journals and OA archives or repositories.
>
> • OA archives or repositories do not perform peer review, but simply make their contents freely available to the world. They may contain unrefereed preprints, refereed postprints, or both. Archives may belong to institutions, such as universities and laboratories, or disciplines, such as physics and economics. Authors may archive their preprints without anyone else's permission, and a majority of journals already permit authors to archive their postprints. When archives comply with the metadata harvesting protocol of the Open Archives Initiative, then they are interoperable and users can find their contents without knowing which archives exist, where they are located, or what they contain. There is now open-source software for building and maintaining OAI-compliant archives and worldwide momentum for using it.

- OA journals perform peer review and then make the approved contents freely available to the world. Their expenses consist of peer review, manuscript preparation, and server space. OA journals pay their bills very much the way broadcast television and radio stations do: those with an interest in disseminating the content pay the production costs upfront so that access can be free of charge for everyone with the right equipment. Sometimes this means that journals have a subsidy from the hosting university or professional society. Sometimes it means that journals charge a processing fee on accepted articles, to be paid by the author or the author's sponsor (employer, funding agency). OA journals that charge processing fees usually waive them in cases of economic hardship. OA journals with institutional subsidies tend to charge no processing fees. OA journals can get by on lower subsidies or fees if they have income from other publications, advertising, priced add-ons, or auxiliary services. Some institutions and consortia arrange fee discounts. Some OA publishers waive the fee for all researchers affiliated with institutions that have purchased an annual membership. There's a lot of room for creativity in finding ways to pay the costs of a peer-reviewed OA journal, and we're far from having exhausted our cleverness and imagination.

(A slightly longer discussion of open access is in Suber's *Open access overview* (Suber 2015), while a much longer (and very worthwhile) discussion is in his book *Open Access* (Suber 2012). Naturally, both of these are open access themselves and can be read freely on the web.)

Open access changes fundamentally the way scholarly work is given to the public. OA is very disruptive of current economic realities, at least in the academic publishing world, with possibly disastrous consequences for for-profit publishers. But this is not the goal of the open access movement, which is instead to make scholarship more widely available and easier to use in the creation of new knowledge. After all we said above in Chapter 4 about free software, it should be clear that OA is an absolutely vital step in the modern evolution of higher education: OA is FLOSS for scholarship, and it is hard to see how it makes sense to use non-OA modes of scholarly publication. Just as the use of nonfree software in the academy is nothing but a failure of academic freedom waiting to happen, non-OA publication of a scholarly work is not much more than scholars signing away their academic freedom, and the freedom of the scholars who will later hope to build on that work. We contend that this violation of freedom only feels less egregious than it really is because we are all used to this punishment. Now that the Information Age allows a fantastic alternative, OA journals and repositories, we should wake up and escape the torture.

There is strong evidence that the OA movement is steadily gaining traction. For example, consider arXiv.org, based at the Cornell University Library. ArXiv.org was founded in 1991 and by the time of this writing hosts more than 1.1 million open access articles in the fields of physics, mathematics, computer science, quantitative biology, quantitative finance, and statistics. Papers on arXiv.org are not peer reviewed, but nevertheless it is immensely important in the intellectual lives of the disciplines it covers. As a slightly extreme and unconventional example, in 2002 and 2003 the Russian mathematician Grisha Perelman put on arXiv.org three of his papers (Perelman (2002), (2003b) and (2003a)) that proved the 100-year-old Poincaré Conjecture—nor did he ever submit them, or other papers based on them, to any traditional journal.[10] The influence of arXiv.org became obvious a few years ago in the submission instructions for well-known scholarly journals in the areas covered by that archive. It used to be that those instructions included a provision excluding papers which had been published elsewhere—physically, or on a public website or in any Internet forum—in a substantially similar form; no longer is there such a provision. The reason simply is that an overwhelming percentage of excellent papers in arXiv.org's subjects are posted there before being submitted to a journal, so the publishers would be excluding the great majority of the important papers they want to be able to publish, unless they changed that exclusion.

Open access is also making inroads by university policies. The leader in this is surely Harvard University, where Peter Suber is the director of both Harvard's Office for Scholarly Communications and its Open Access Project. The faculty of the School of Arts and Sciences voted unanimously to give their institution a nonexclusive, irrevocable right to distribute their scholarly articles for any non-commercial purpose. This was then followed by similar policies at the eight other schools (academic units) at Harvard. These works are then put in an open archive called *Digital Access to Scholarship at Harvard (DASH)* and so are available to be indexed, searched, and viewed by anyone on the web. This approach is obviously in contradiction with publishers' *embargo* policies, whereby only the publisher, through its pay-walled portal, may distribute any versions of articles for some fixed period of time—anything in the range of one to three years is common. Harvard has used its prestige to negotiate special exceptions to embargo policies, sometimes pays an extra fee on behalf of its authors, and also clearly encourages its authors to avoid journals where there is recalcitrant policy or high fee.

Few institutions have enough prestige to engage successfully in such negotiations with publishers or deep enough pockets to cover many OA fees, but all institutions can form consortia which start to have similar possibilities. In any case, if academics as a community vote with their feet in favor of for-profit journal publishers that have strong open access policies or use, whenever possible, the new purely OA journals, then we can work to end the evil of non-OA scholarship. In the end, just like DRM, non-OA scholarly publication will almost certainly die out—we just need to hurry this process as much as we can. The Harvard Office for Scholarly Communication has many helpful resources, such as sample university OA policies, at its website osc.hul.harvard.edu/policies/.

Fair Use and the Creative Commons

Free use of parts of a copyrighted work is sometimes permitted by a tenet of copyright law called *fair use* (*fair dealing* in Commonwealth countries is quite similar, although different in some important respects). Fair use is defined in 17 U.S. Code §107, which states:

> Notwithstanding the provisions of sections 106 and 106A, the fair use of a copyrighted work, including such use by reproduction in copies or phonorecords or by any other means specified by that section, for purposes such as criticism, comment, news reporting, teaching (including multiple copies for classroom use), scholarship, or research, is not an infringement of copyright. In determining whether the use made of a work in any particular case is a fair use the factors to be considered shall include–
>
> **(1)** the purpose and character of the use, including whether such use is of a commercial nature or is for nonprofit educational purposes;
> **(2)** the nature of the copyrighted work;
> **(3)** the amount and substantiality of the portion used in relation to the copyrighted work as a whole; and
> **(4)** the effect of the use upon the potential market for or value of the copyrighted work.
>
> The fact that a work is unpublished shall not itself bar a finding of fair use if such finding is made upon consideration of all the above factors.

We think it is a good idea for any academic (perhaps any person who wants to be active on the World Wide Web) to know a bit about fair use—in our experience, professors are overly cautious about using the fair use exception in their teaching. But our use of Suber's *Very Brief Introduction* seems to fall afoul of provisions (1) (this book is not being used in a narrowly educational, non-profit context) and (3) (we quoted nearly the whole thing). Nevertheless, we are free to use the quote as we did because Suber released that article with a *creative commons* license.

Look back at the ideas we described as underlying both FLOSS and OA, including those impulses for sharing, encouragement of re-use and remix, and (viral) requirement of the openness of derivative works. A natural question about these ideas is, why not make a careful legal way to apply them to any copyrightable work? When an author wants specifically to abjure the rights of copyright-holder for control, and also to force this freedom to be viral, that author needs something like the GNU Public License but generalized away from the software to which the GPL applies. Acting on this idea, Larry Lessig, Hal Abelson, and Eric Eldred (a lawyer, a computer scientist, and an activist) founded the non-profit organization Creative Commons, creativecommons.org, in 2001.

Creative Commons has written a suite of licenses, now in their fourth iteration, which provide legal details for licenses with various versions of rights. Taken from the page creativecommons.org/licenses/, they are:

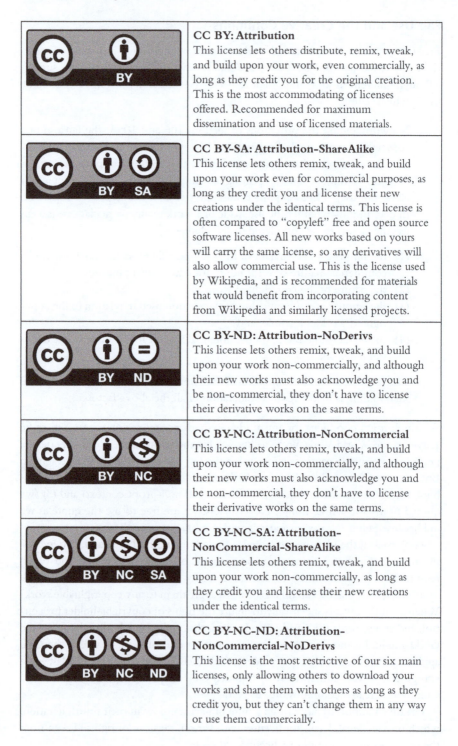

CC BY: Attribution

This license lets others distribute, remix, tweak, and build upon your work, even commercially, as long as they credit you for the original creation. This is the most accommodating of licenses offered. Recommended for maximum dissemination and use of licensed materials.

CC BY-SA: Attribution–ShareAlike

This license lets others remix, tweak, and build upon your work even for commercial purposes, as long as they credit you and license their new creations under the identical terms. This license is often compared to "copyleft" free and open source software licenses. All new works based on yours will carry the same license, so any derivatives will also allow commercial use. This is the license used by Wikipedia, and is recommended for materials that would benefit from incorporating content from Wikipedia and similarly licensed projects.

CC BY-ND: Attribution–NoDerivs

This license lets others remix, tweak, and build upon your work non-commercially, and although their new works must also acknowledge you and be non-commercial, they don't have to license their derivative works on the same terms.

CC BY-NC: Attribution–NonCommercial

This license lets others remix, tweak, and build upon your work non-commercially, and although their new works must also acknowledge you and be non-commercial, they don't have to license their derivative works on the same terms.

CC BY-NC-SA: Attribution–NonCommercial–ShareAlike

This license lets others remix, tweak, and build upon your work non-commercially, as long as they credit you and license their new creations under the identical terms.

CC BY-NC-ND: Attribution–NonCommercial–NoDerivs

This license is the most restrictive of our six main licenses, only allowing others to download your works and share them with others as long as they credit you, but they can't change them in any way or use them commercially.

Notice that putting a CC license on a copyrightable work is not the same thing as that work being in the *public domain*, meaning that anyone is free to use it absolutely, however they want. An otherwise copyrightable work "falls[11] into the public domain" when the term of copyright expires. Works are also in the public domain when the author announces their intention to place it there, and in a few other specific situations. (One useful such is that all works produced by the U.S. federal government are automatically placed in the public domain—this applies to any document, image, or other digital data which is on a federal government website, absent any specific assertion of copyright.) CC licenses instead use the power that comes with copyright ownership to allow certain uses and to forbid others. If you release a work with a CC license, you are absolutely not giving up the copyright on that work, not putting it in the public domain,

CC licenses are now widely used and recognized. According to the organization's history web page creativecommons.org/about/history/, there were a total of 1 billion works with CC licenses in 2015. YouTube, Flickr, and other data sharing sites now offer CC licenses as an option for users when they upload their media. Wikipedia requires all entries to be under a CC license, while the content on Wikimedia Commons, a digital media-sharing wiki run by the Wikimedia Foundation (which also runs Wikipedia), must all be under some form of sharing license such as a CC license, public domain, or a few other special licenses.

In the university context, scholars should try whenever possible to put a CC license on their works. This certainly includes articles going on open access archives or in OA journals, but also materials posted on the web or distributed in other ways, pedagogical materials, and any small write-ups of scholarly work. Unless you are hoping to turn a particular written work into a piece of a profit-making enterprise, the academic ethic is to share, and to expect that works inspired by yours will also be shared. This is what CC licenses are for, to give your works the legal status of full-fledged members of the academic ideas commons.

Information Wants to Be Free: Open Textbooks

We noted above that the subscription costs of many journals are growing at an astonishing rate, but the situation is far worse for textbooks. Two different studies, (Perry 2012) and (Popken 2015), found that the cost of textbooks has increased either 864 or 1,041 percent from the late 1970s to the early 2010s. In either case, this rate far exceeds the costs increase for health care, homes, the consumer price index, university tuition, and so on. The National Association of College Stores *Higher Education Retail Market Facts & Figures* (NACS 2015) show a steady decrease in the amount of money students spend on required course materials such as textbooks from $701 in 2007/8 to $563 in 2014/15, although their methodology does not seem particularly accurate—and the College Board estimates (in their college cost FAQ at bigfuture.collegeboard.org/pay-for-college/college-costs/quick-guide-college-costs) instead that an undergraduate at a four-year public university will need $1,200 for books and supplies.

The decline in student expenditures found by the NACS is likely to be due to students choosing, under economic pressure, not to buy some required textbooks new and instead to buy a used copy or to download a pirated copy. A survey of students conducted by The U.S. PIRG Education Fund and The Student PIRGs found that a majority of students did not buy at least one textbook because of the cost, although a majority was somewhat or significantly concerned about the consequences of this choice on their studies (Senack 2014).

In science, technology, engineering, and mathematics (STEM), where many of the textbooks cost in the range $200–$350, it is not uncommon that several students in every class are unable to afford the book each semester. This is obviously an enormous obstacle to success. Furthermore, in subjects such as mathematics and physics where much of the material we teach is from many decades to several centuries old, the textbooks come out in new editions every three years, or so—at which point the market in used copies of the older edition disappears. Note that the changes from edition to edition tend to be quite minor, although they always include a few minor changes to the homework exercises, so that student cannot possibly successfully do the required homework sets with the older edition.

In this situation, the publishers of the most popular textbooks are using their market dominance to reap a profit which is not really justified. Why do faculty accept this state of affairs? We must admit there is something of a question of *cui bono:* the decision about which textbook to use is made by faculty who get free copies from the publisher and often other perks such as PowerPoint decks to lecture from, worked-answer keys, test banks, volumes of worksheets and classroom activities, and invitations to professional development events, not to mention a great deal of personalized attention from the publishers' reps. It is only the students who pay the price.

The dominant neoliberal ideology of the moment also has an impact on faculty decisions for textbooks. Shouldn't an author get a nice profit from a successful book, even if we did not choose this career for its financial prospects, and even though the material in that successful textbook is perfectly standard and we write most of it down in our own words every time we prepare our class notes? And shouldn't the students expect to pay more for a high-quality book? Its high price should be a guarantee of quality, shouldn't it?

Finally, many faculty members who write textbooks are probably hoping that their book might be the one which somehow takes off, causing a sudden financial windfall which was hoped-for but certainly not expected. Like winning the lottery, this would seem to be a random stroke of good luck, about which one does not stop to consider all the unlucky peons (the students, in this case) who are paying for that jackpot.

Like the situations we have already seen to do with free *vs* nonfree software and overpriced scholarly journals, there is good news here, enabled by information technology and networks. The FLOSS typesetting and electronic publishing tools which we have mentioned above make easy the production of pedagogical materials with extremely high production values. Students today are used to reading on their screens, and nearly all of them have at least a smartphone with which they can access an electronic book posted on the Internet.

Textbooks produced and distributed in this way—and, crucially, released with creative commons licenses—have come to be called *open textbooks*. A number of collective efforts have been made for open textbooks, such as OpenStax College at Rice University, openstaxcollege.org, the Center for Open Education at the University of Minnesota, open.umn.edu, and numerous others.

Often those larger, institutionalized efforts have peer-reviewed open textbooks. The advantage of peer review is, of course, quality, and also easier acceptance by university faculty. But most lecture notes that faculty create when preparing their classes are never seen by anyone else, so a more Wikipedia-like, hand-rolled approach is also reasonable. The *artisanal open textbook strategy*, we might call it, can produce extremely customized textbooks that do exactly what the professor wants and the students need. Whether this approach makes sense comes around again to a consideration of marginal costs.

As we have already seen, the IT infrastructure is already present (in the Global North, at least). Powerful and easy-to-use FLOSS software is also available. Most experienced professors have a fairly good idea of what they want their students to have available as a textbook. Quite a bit of this material will be in the public domain, or useable for reasons of fair use. Other widely known (in the field) material can be written down quickly by the experienced professor and incorporated into an open textbook without fear of copyright violation so long as it is expressed in that professor's own words—remember, copyright is on the *expression*, not the *idea*. (For that matter, there is also an exception in copyright law for matters that have essentially only one way to be expressed. For example, a new textbook can state the Pythagorean Theorem in a standard, traditional form, because there is essentially only one way to state that theorem.[12])

All that is missing before open textbooks become the dominant, widespread standard—aside from changing the neoliberal mindset we mentioned above—is a public archive of open textbook chapters and sections under CC license, with a small amount of software to help put together these fragments into an official-looking book. The user (professor) would select a rich collection of such fragments, write a few new ones, and/or modify some old ones to say exactly what they wanted. At that point, students in the class could read the book online, or get a printed copy which would cost merely a few dollars. (The advantage of the online version, by the way, would be that it could be modified, expanded, and adapted as the course progressed.)

Even before this archive and supporting software is available, it is still not all that difficult to make an open textbook for a class. Here's one such story: one of us (JP) was switched onto a Number Theory class at the last minute a few semesters ago, by which point it was hard to get a commercial textbook in time. In any case, the commercial textbook which is often used is about $170 in our bookstore, for a book filled with results which are mostly two hundred years old. So I simply typed each week's lecture notes in TeX (the FLOSS mathematical typesetting program mentioned in Chapter 4) and pointed out to the students sections of this gradually growing book on my website. It helped me get started that I had an already existing number theory textbook, released by a Lebanese mathematician named Wissam Raji under a CC license, to work with, although by the middle of the semester I had gotten good enough at producing my own sections that I didn't need Raji's book very much at all.

The second time I taught the same class, I was able to polish the book quite a bit more, and add to it a detailed new section of modern applications of number theory. The book, which I called *Yet Another Introductory Number Theory Textbook* (Poritz 2014) is free, under a CC license, from my website, and costs less than $7 for a physical copy from an on-demand printing service.

It was only worth giving the detail on this particular example to show how the marginal cost of educational materials can drop nearly to zero for our students, albeit at a slightly higher cost in terms of faculty labor. But due to the quickly falling marginal costs of infrastructure and similar drop in the labor required to produce free, customized open textbooks as we get more experience and better tools and resources, the era of zero-marginal-cost pedagogical materials should soon be here.

One cute thing about a successful open textbook epoch would be that it would give some solid reality to the expression "Information wants to be free." That expression has been something of a rallying cry in the free software, open access, and creative commons movements.[13] It would be particularly nice to make this cry true for some of the most deserving and debt-burdened Americans today: students in higher education.

Notes

1 Recall that the *marginal cost* of a product is the cost of one additional unit of the product, after some number of units have already been produced. The *marginal cost curve* is the graph of the marginal cost as a function of total number of units.

2 A *kilobyte (KB)* is 1024 bytes—so, approximately a thousand bytes, hence the Greek root *kilo*—where a *byte* is 8 bits. Why 1024? Well, it's 2^{10}, "don't you see? (You ask a silly question, you get a silly answer.)" (Lehrer 1965)

3 A *megabyte (MB)* is 1048576 (which is 2^{20}) bytes, or 1024 KB—so, approximately a million bytes.

4 1*kbps* is one thousand bits per second. Yes: 1000, not 1024, which we can tell since it is a *k* and not a *K*.

5 1*mbps* is one million bits per second. 1000000, not 1048576, because it is *m* and not *M*.

6 A *gigabyte (GB)* is 2^{30} bytes or 1024 MB—about a thousand million bytes.

7 A *petabyte (PB)* is 2^{50} bytes or 1024^2 GB, more than a million gigabytes.

8 This is probably a controversial statement in these anti-intellectual times. But if we believe that education is in any way a driver of macroeconomic success—as, for example, Goldin & Katz (2009) demonstrates in glorious detail—and if education has any value for our students in their future employment prospects, then surely those who know the facts and have the skills in sufficient measure to teach them would be even more attractive in the business world.

9 See Houghton, et al. (2009) for more information.

10 Perelman is a bit of a special case, it must be admitted. He is an almost stereotypically unconventional mathematical genius who, for example, refused the Fields Medal

(considered to be the Nobel Prize of mathematics) because he was not interested in money or fame.

11 Copyright lawyers think of it as "falling," as in "from grace."

12 Well, in any case statements of the Pythagorean Theorem would have fallen into the public domain long ago, since at this moment in history we are at life of the author plus more than 2,000 years. But the exception for matters with essentially unique expressions holds also for more recently written works, such as a new theorem proven and published in only the last few years.

13 Although, see Doctorow (2014) for an interesting critique: information doesn't want anything, including freedom, Doctorow points out—but people do.

9

CONCLUSION

Higher Education in a Digital Age

The Purpose of a University

> Institutions of higher education are conducted for the common good and not to further the interest of either the individual teacher or the institution as a whole. The common good depends upon the free search for truth and its free exposition.
>
> Academic freedom is essential to these purposes and applies to both teaching and research. Freedom in research is fundamental to the advancement of truth. Academic freedom in its teaching aspect is fundamental for the protection of the rights of the teacher in teaching and of the student to freedom in learning.
>
> *(AAUP 1940)*

The question with which we began—"Is your university actually an institution of higher education?"—is built on the foundations laid in this passage from the AAUP's *1940 Statement of Principles on Academic Freedom and Tenure.*

The freedom of the teacher to teach and the freedom of the student to learn are both part of a direct relationship between teacher and student. When technology is inserted into this relationship, it can enrich the interaction by allowing broader and more flexible accessibility, enabling new modes of interaction (such as fora and social media), incorporating new scholarly resources, and so on. Just as the Internet lowers barriers between producers and consumers of products and services, information technology can disintermediate students, teachers, and the subject matter of their common pedagogical purpose.

But no IT can meaningfully replace either side of this relationship: ***Every real student deserves individual attention from, and interaction with, a real teacher.*** Education is not really happening if it is merely an exercise of regurgitating facts and figures, or reproducing a physical or mental motion in exactly the same manner as a model, or if it is a task which a machine could do. Real education, pursued by real students, requires critical thinking and creativity, and therefore cannot be evaluated or nurtured by anyone other than another human being who understands and can do those original things, adapting and responding to the student's unexpected creative steps: a real teacher.

We have seen failures at both ends of this spectrum. Education in some disciplines (such as, sadly, the all too common "drill-and-kill" classes in STEM) has been so reduced to uncritical conditioning of the students that it can be "taught" by computer programs such as unbundled interactive tools in MOOCs or automated grading systems used to enable overfull classes of overworked, underpaid adjuncts. At the other end, for classes which do teach problem solving, creativity, and critical thinking, any automated grading system which actually worked would be able to pass the Turing test. So, if you like, we could replace "real student" and "real teacher" in this discussion by "Turing-certified, human-level intelligence (either human or artificial) playing the roles of student and teacher."

Implicit here is an idea of the importance of class sizes—which is consistent with the research literature on the subject, see for example (Finn 2002), (Krueger 2003), or many others. If students deserve interaction with their teachers and the teachers are human (and not the fictional human-level AIs), you cannot scale the classroom to become, say, "massive" without also scaling the real human attention given on the teacher side—at least not if you want what happens in that massive classroom still to be worthy of the name "education." (If all you're after is a virtual community of self-motivated autodidacts, like some sort of Reddit-enabled neighborhood book club, then by all means ignore this argument.)

Faculty Working Conditions Are Student Learning Conditions

This old saying in faculty circles is merely a tautology. After all, both groups are in the same room together during conventional classrooms. However, this is not necessarily true in an online environment. With faculty and students in different places, an adjunct instructor might live in squalor while an affluent college student could be logging into class from a lavish dormitory full of the kinds of inducements needed to get rich kids to enroll in college—like climbing walls and all-organic menus in the cafeteria. Nevertheless, even in an online environment, students face learning conditions that derive directly from the position of their teacher. If an instructor is paid so little they have no incentive to work hard on the class and no time for interaction with the students (because of the heavy class load required to make a full salary) that affects student learning. If an instructor is restricted in the kinds of subjects they can bring up during class, it affects student learning. And most importantly for purposes of this analysis, if faculty members do not have the opportunity to convey the skills they learned in graduate school because the educational technology they're using narrows the definition of what education is, then that affects student learning, too.

We think it is worth adding a second clause to the old tautology: *Professors' working conditions are their students' learning conditions; professors without autonomy and agency cannot teach those characteristics*. Our addition might seem like wishful thinking. In fact, Stanley Fish (Fish 2014) criticizes this idea, saying that it is perfectly possible to educate for freedom while suffering under tyranny (we paraphrase). But we disagree with Fish.

Samuel Bowles and Gintis's pillar of the sociology of education *Schooling in Capitalist America: Educational Reform and the Contradictions of Economic Life* (Bowles and Gintis 1976) is much more persuasive. Bowles and Gintis describe what they call the *correspondence principle* whereby the social relations in schools correspond to those in the workspace:

> [T]he educational system operates ... through a close correspondence between the social relationships which govern personal interaction in the work place and the social relationships of the educational system. Specifically, the relationships of authority and control between administrators and teachers, teachers and students, students and students, and students and their work replicate the hierarchical division of labor which dominates the work place. Power is organized along vertical lines of authority from administration to faculty to student body; students have a degree of control over their curriculum comparable to that of the worker over the content of his job. The motivational system of the school, involving as it does grades and other external rewards and the threat of failure rather than the intrinsic social benefits of the process of education (learning) or its tangible outcome (knowledge), mirrors closely the role of wages and the specter of unemployment in the motivation of workers.

This structural, cultural theory of correspondence itself mirrors the more economic versions we discussed in Chapter 6. There, we saw that Taylorist structures within the academy serve to limit the creativity and innovation which are the only ways students can be prepared to be anything other than robot-like (Taylorist) unthinking workers.

On a much more concrete, practical level, experienced university professors know that a large part—a majority?—of what we are doing in the classroom is acting as role models. We are living examples of how someone can confront the intellectual challenges of the material and also live well within the organizational, procedural, and bureaucratic constraints of available learning resources, information technology, scholarly products, and so on. When a prominent female figure in academia says she is not good at numbers, it does damage to the cause of gender equality in STEM. In the same way, whenever a university professor says "I don't get to decide that" in class, or simply makes it clear by an action, damage is done to the students' understanding of the possibility and importance of autonomy and agency.

An easy solution to prevent this problem is simply to return (again) to the definition of academic freedom from about 100 years ago. It reminds us that faculty should have that freedom "in relation to purely scientific and educational questions, the primary responsibility," in the words of the *1915 Declaration of Principles on Academic Freedom and Academic Tenure*. In the last generation, information technology has become an indispensable part of the scientific (for which, read the 1915 language as meaning "scholarly") and educational work that a university does. That's why faculty should have primary responsibility in making information technology decisions. It is a vital part of their educational responsibilities.

Instead, the Internet has become an avenue for administrators, staff, and governing boards to seize greater control of every aspect of university life. Because of a culture which expects websites only to be concerned with marketing, universities think that they need to have "consistent branding on [their] web presence" (as a vice president at our campus said recently). Instead, faculty know that a useful university website has lots of actual information, not so much advertising—information *is* marketing in the higher education business. Similarly, where consumers outside of academia are used to using commercial IT devices and software, scholars are used to FLOSS—or if not, they are certainly aware of the Enlightenment values which underlie FLOSS. Therefore they can steer campus IT strategy and resources in the direction of FLOSS because it fits their world so much better than nonfree software does. But both of these examples only work if faculty members are given the primary role in IT decisions which the tenets of academic freedom do in fact require, although no one seems to have noticed this.

The fact that even the most cash-starved universities always seem to have the money to buy expensive, corporate edtech demonstrates something we've heard often from AAUP national officers who have studied such matters: **Your university is not broke.** How many pet projects has your president and board of governors been able to fund over the course of your time there when such a project fit their priorities? Decisions about funding in general and campus IT in particular are ideological and political more than they are economic. The federal government of the United States spends money on defense and on bailing out big banks, but not on making university cheap or even free. State governments in the U.S. also prioritize tax cuts over funding of state universities.

University systems prioritize building new sports stadiums, costing hundreds of millions of dollars, over spending on academic programs. Individual university campuses choose to spend more every year on administrative bloat, while adjuncts are not given a living wage and no faculty member is given a cost-of-living adjustment. And those individual administrators often choose to pay expensive consultants rather than to develop internal expertise, or even to take advantage of that expertise which probably exists on the campus (often among the faculty).

In fact, *these decisions are largely ideological and political.* We have already seen how the advancement of a Taylorist agenda and its necessary deskilling was such an existential threat to the creative and educational missions of higher education that the whole concept of academic freedom had to be invented as a defense. Today, neoliberalism is a much more modern, dominant politico-economic ideology. One consequence of neoliberalism for higher education is a state of permanent austerity.

While particularly acute at state-run universities, neoliberalism is actually important everywhere because the growing divide between rich and poor threatens the availability of any college whatsoever for an increasing number of people worldwide. Educational technology dovetails beautifully with an agenda of permanent austerity because it holds the potential (but as we have seen, seldom the reality) of saving universities money. Administrators can therefore claim to pass the savings from education technology on to students, even as further budget cuts only drive up their tuition bills more.

We think there's a better way. As an institution, a university should not lock itself into large nonfree systems such as monolithic commercial LMSs. In short, **Edtech wants to be free.** By this, we mean edtech must serve the needs of academic freedom and the choices of the experts, the scholar-teachers. This amounts to a buffet model of educational technology. Instead of simply imposing a single system of classroom management or e-mail or even a single way to access the Internet, the job of campus IT shops is to help faculty, students, and staff choose from a diverse selection of IT offerings available on the open Internet or through inexpensive university-purchased licenses. This will allow every actor at the university to find the best programs that support their pedagogy or their learning.

In each course, professors could then create an augmented or entirely virtual classroom that fits their specific needs, free of administrative interference, by employing the buffet philosophy. Many of the tools they would choose would be FLOSS, but even nonfree software should be available to those who judge them to be the best solutions to the pedagogical and scholarly problems they confront. Certainly, there are challenges to running your class using commercial tools (even free ones) created by for-profit enterprises, but if those companies do not dictate the way you teach, then it need not violate academic freedom. For example, by spreading your technological choices across different providers, changes for the worse in one of them will not be likely to affect the way you teach the rest of your course.

This isn't like the current reality, in which IT staff are as often an obstacle as an aide to finding the best solutions which use IT. They usually enforce the use of the particular (nonfree) tools which have been purchased or licensed, with minimal regard to whether they actually solve the real problems of education and research. It is unclear to us whether a change of perspective for campus IT shops is at all possible with such shops sitting where they currently do in campus organization charts. That's why we suggested giving the decision-makers in those shops tenure and the academic freedom that comes with it.

But it is not only IT staff today who have work to do. When one of us (JP) was a graduate student, he asked a senior professor in his department why that professor did not use the excellent free software tool TeX to typeset his own research papers. This scholar was famously picky about how the complex diagrams in his papers appeared in print, but he achieved this by writing them out long-hand and going through endless cycles of correction and adjustment with publishers. Most math and science papers then, and essentially all today, are delivered to journal publishers in camera-ready form, using TeX, but this professor explained that "when computers all speak the same language, then I'll learn how to use them."

This attitude is no longer acceptable in academia, although sadly it is not unusual. Under our vision of a technological buffet, *It is the responsibility of the academic faculty to keep current on technological developments, no matter how far outside their comfort zone such learning may be.* Don't let yourself be railroaded into using clunky, expensive, illogical learning management systems. Don't let yourselves be bamboozled by a company handing out a free, inferior product—and do understand the advantages of FLOSS. Faculty teach much more complicated things every day and expect their students to struggle through to mastery. Teacher-scholars also do research as an ongoing part of their lives, one of the benefits of which is said to be that it reminds the professionals what it is like for their students to work hard, to try again and again, until they can move from the painful state of not understanding to the blissful one of understanding. The same lesson should also apply in the much simpler arena of learning about the tools for scholarship and pedagogy of their chosen disciplines.

It is well past time for faculty to accept responsibility for our technological higher educational future. The question that remains to be resolved is whether that future will be imposed from the top down, the outside in or from the bottom up. Every application designed by Silicon Valley is not necessarily inferior. Every decision made by a university provost or president is not necessarily all about money. Likewise, every choice a faculty member makes is not necessarily in their students' best interests. However, given a choice between these three groups as to who gets to drive the higher education train we trust faculty the most because they are experts in education by virtue of their collective experience. Faculty autonomy promotes a natural experiment in pedagogical matters in an environment where different disciplines and different people within those disciplines will have different definitions of success. We think everybody concerned in higher education should embrace those differences.

Caring, knowledgeable faculty members possessing academic freedoms have long been able to create engaging, intellectually rigorous classes. Adding technology to these classes—or even rebuilding them entirely with technology or online—does not change that ability, so long as the technology does not end professors' creative freedom. The way we see to achieve this is to vest the decision-making authority in the faculty, to offer them a rich technological buffet from which to choose, to expect them to educate themselves so as to be able to make informed choices, and to steer clear of one-size-fits-all solutions imposed for non-academic reasons.

The roots of academic freedom go back one hundred years as a defense of the common good in universities against the onslaught of scientific management's deskilling, and then also back thirty years to the concept of academic freedom for software and information—FLOSS and the creative commons. When edtech start-ups rise and fall and the most widely used styles for websites change between the time we hand out syllabi on the first day of class and when we collect the final exams on the last, or so it seems, it feels odd that the principles faculty value and the battles we fight are decades, if not a century, old. But these principles and values have stood the academic community in good stead for much longer, actually, and we can continue to use them today. This book has looked for some truths in the arena of the academy's survival in the face of truly revolutionary changes in information technology. While these changes endanger the fundamental values of higher education, they also open positive new opportunities.

Our hope is that the detailed explorations in the preceding chapters, and the more focused principles in this concluding one, will help you search for truth, freely express what you find, and prioritize the common good, both within and without the world of higher education.

APPENDIX: JONATHANS' LAWS

1. Every real student deserves individual attention from, and interaction with, a real teacher.

2. Professors' working conditions are their students' learning conditions; professors without autonomy and agency cannot teach those characteristics.

3. Since your university is not broke, the root causes of IT decisions are ideological and political, not economic.

4. Edtech wants to be free; FLOSS is the best way to build that freedom.

5. It is the responsibility of the academic faculty to keep current on technological developments, no matter how far outside their comfort zone such learning may be.

BIBLIOGRAPHY

Internet User's Glossary (1993). Request for Comments (RFC) 1392. January 1993, rfc-editor. org/rfc/rfc1392.txt, Accessed: 3 January 2016.

AAUP (1915) *Declaration of Principles on Academic Freedom and Academic Tenure.* American Association of University Professors. aaup.org/NR/rdonlyres/A6520A9D-0A9A-47B3-B550-C006B5B224E7/0/1915Declaration.pdf, Accessed: 8 November 2015.

AAUP (1940) *Statement of Principles on Academic Freedom and Tenure.* American Association of University Professors. aaup.org/report/1940-statement-principles-academic-freedom-and-tenure, Accessed: 9 January 2016.

AAUP (2013a) *Academic Freedom and Electronic Communications.* American Association of University Professors. aaup.org/report/academic-freedom-and-electronic-communications, Accessed: 28 December 2015.

AAUP (2013b). *Statement on the Freedom to Teach.* American Association of University Professors. 7 November 2013, aaup.org/news/statement-freedom-teach, Accessed: 19 January 2016.

AAUP (2014). *Background Facts on Contingent Faculty.* American Association of University Professors. aaup.org/issues/contingency/background-facts, Accessed: 16 November 2014.

ADS (2011). *"App" Voted 2010 Word of the Year by the American Dialect Society (Updated).* American Dialect Society. americandialect.org/app-voted-2010-word-of-the-year-by-the-american-dialect-society-updated, Accessed: 24 December 2014.

Agarwal, A. (2015a). *Expect MOOCs to Get More Personal.* LinkedIn Pulse, 6 April 2015, linkedin.com/pulse/expect-moocs-get-more-personal-anant-agarwal, Accessed: 27 December 2015.

Agarwal, A. (2015b). *Reimagine Freshman Year with the Global Freshman Academy.* edX blog, 22 April 2015, blog.edx.org/reimagine-freshman-year-global-freshman, Accessed: 26 December 2015.

ALA (2004). *Core Values of Librarianship.* American Library Association. adopted 29 June 2004, ala.org/advocacy/intfreedom/statementspols/corevalues, Accessed: 27 January 2016.

ALEKS (2016). *Math Help (ALEKS).* McGraw-Hill Higher Education. highered.mheducation. com/sites/0070524076/student_view0/math_help__aleks_.html, Accessed: 20 January 2016.

Anderson, J. et al. (2012). *The Future of Higher Education*. Pew Research Center. pewinternet. org/2012/07/27/the-future-of-higher-education/, Accessed: 25 December 2015.

Annenberg (2013). *Is Online Privacy Over?* Center for the Digital Future, USC Annenberg School for Communication and Journalism, 22 April 2013, www.digitalcenter.org/ online-privacy-and-millennials-0413, Accessed: 27 January 2016.

Anonymous (2015). 'Treadmill to oblivion'. *Inside Higher Education,* 11 May 2015, inside-highered.com/advice/2015/05/11/essay-instructor-who-has-taught-adjunct-25-years, Accessed: 25 December 2015.

Asimov, N. (2013). 'UC online courses fail to lure outsiders'. *San Francisco Chronicle,* 22 February 2013, sfgate.com/education/article/UC-online-courses-fail-to-lure-outsiders-4173639.php, Accessed: 16 November 2014.

Au, W. (2011). 'Teaching under the new Taylorism: high-stakes testing and the standardization of the 21st century curriculum'. *Journal of Curriculum Studies* **43**(1):25–45.

Auletta, K. (2012). 'Get Rich U'. *The New Yorker* **30**:38–47.

Bernstein, S. (2014). 'University of California's Napolitano joins skeptics over online courses'. *Reuters* 24 March 2014, reuters.com/article/2014/03/25/us-usa-california-napolitano-idUSBREA2O02R20140325, Accessed: 25 December 2015.

Berrett, D. (2010). 'ESU Professor Suspended for Comments Made On Facebook Page'. *Pocono Record,* 26 February 2010, poconorecord.com/article/20100226/NEWS/2260344, Accessed: 28 December 2015.

Boie, J. and H. Grassegger. (2015). *MOOCs and Privacy, German Fears about Online Student Data.* Worldcrunch, 11 December 2015, worldcrunch.com/culture-society/moocs-and-privacy-german-fears-about-online-student-data/c3s20245/, Accessed: 26 December 2015.

Borland, J. (2003). *Court Blocks Security Conference Talk.* CNET, 15 April 2003, cnet.com/ news/court-blocks-security-conference-talk, Accessed: 2 January 2016.

Bousquet, M. and C. Nelson (2008). *How the University Works: Higher Education and the Low-wage Nation.* NYU Press, New York, NY, USA.

Bowen, W. G. (2001). *At a Slight Angle to the Universe: The University in a Digitized, Commercialized Age.* Association of Research Libraries. arl.org/storage/documents/ publications/arl-br-216.pdf, Accessed 25 December 2015.

Bowen, W. G. (2015a). *Higher Eduation in the Digital Age.* Princeton University Press, Princeton, NJ, USA.

Bowen, W. G. (2015b). '*Higher education in the digital age*', chap. Discussion by Andrew Delbanco. Princeton University Press, Princeton, NJ, USA.

Bowles, S. and H. Gintis (1976). *Schooling in Capitalist America.* Basic Books, New York, NY, USA.

Boyer, C. B. and U. C. Merzbach (2011). *A History of Mathematics.* John Wiley & Sons, New York, NY, USA.

Bray, H. (2002). 'Cyber chief speaks on data network security'. *The Boston Globe,* 17 October 2002.

Brown, I. (2013). 'Will NSA revelations lead to the Balkanisation of the internet?'. *The Guardian,* 1 November 2013, theguardian.com/world/2013/nov/01/nsa-revelations-balkanisation-internet, Accessed: 25 January 2016.

Burt, R. S. (2004). 'Structural holes and good ideas'. *American Journal of Sociology* **110**(2): 349–399.

Butler, S. M. (2015). *How Google and Coursera May Upend the Traditional College Degree.* Brookings Tech Tank. 23 February 2015, brookings.edu/blogs/techtank/posts/2015/ 02/23-mooc-google-coursera-butler, Accessed: 27 December 2015.

Byrnes, N. (2015). 'Uber for education'. *MIT Technology Review,* 27 July 2015, technology review.com/news/539106/uber-for-education/, 27 December 2015.

Carey, K. (2015). *The End of College: Creating the Future of Learning and the University of Everywhere*. Riverhead Books, New York, NY, USA.

Carr, N. (2014). *The Glass Cage: Automation and US*. W.W. Norton, New York, NY, USA.

Carr, N. (2015). *Media Takes Command*. Rough Type. roughtype.com/?p=6172, Accessed: 25 December 2015.

Cassidy, J. (2015). 'College calculus: What's the real value of higher education?' *The New Yorker,* 7 September 2015, newyorker.com/magazine/2015/09/07/college-calculus, Accessed: 19 January 2016.

Cegłowski, M. (2015). 'Haunted By Data' talk presented 1 October 2015 at the *Strata+Hadoop World* Conference in New York City, video youtube.com/watch?v=GAXLHM-1Psk, transcript idlewords.com/talks/haunted_by_data.htm, Accessed: 27 Jan 2016.

Chafkin, M. (2013). 'Udacity's Sebastian Thrun, godfather of free online education, changes course'. *Fast Company* **14**. fastcompany.com/3021473/udacity-sebastian-thrun-uphill-climb, Accessed: 26 December 2015.

Cheathem, M. (2013). *Selling the Matrix Revolution in Higher Education*. Jacksonian America, 11 March 2013, jacksonianamerica.com/2013/03/11/selling-the-matrix-revolution-in-higher-education/, Accessed: 27 December 2015.

Chomsky, N. (2002). *Syntactic Structure*. Walter de Gruyter, 2nd edn, Berlin.

Christensen, C. (2013). *The Innovator's Dilemma: When New Technologies Cause Great Firms to Fail*. Harvard Business Review Press, Boston, MA, USA.

Christensen, C. M. and H. J. Eyring (2011). *The Innovative University: Changing the DNA of Higher Education from the Inside Out*. Jossey-Bass, San Francisco, CA, USA.

Cicero, L. (2012). *Universities Suffering from Near-fatal 'Cost Disease'*. Stanford University. 12 October 2012, news.stanford.edu/news/2012/october/tanner-lecture-one-101212.html, Accessed: 20 July 2015.

College of Natural Science University of Texas (2011). 'About Quest'. getquest.cns.utexas.edu/about-quest, Accessed: 27 December 2015.

Cottom, T. M. (2015). *Everything but the Burden: Publics, Public Scholarship, and Institutions*. tressiemc. 12 May 2015, tressiemc.com/2015/05/12/everything-but-the-burden-publics-public-scholarship-and-institutions/, Accessed: 28 December 2015.

Craig, R. (2015). *College Disrupted: The Great Unbundling of Higher Education*. Palgrave Macmillan, New York, NY, USA.

Crawford, S. P. (2013). *Captive Audience: The Telecom Industry and Monopoly Power in the New Gilded Age*. Yale University Press, New Haven, CT, USA.

Daly, E. (2014). 'How many people are watching Netflix?' *Radio Times,* 27 February 2014, radiotimes.com/news/2014-02027/how-many-people-are-watching-netflix, Accessed: 16 January 2016.

Davidson, J. (2014). 'The 7 social media mistakes most likely to cost you a job'. *Money* 16 October 2014, time.com/money/3510967/jobvite-social-media-profiles-job-applicants/, Accessed: 28 December 2015.

DiCerbo, K. E. and J. T. Behrens (2014). *Impacts of the Digital Ocean on Education*. Pearson. research.pearson.com/content/plc/prkc/uk/open-ideas/en/articles/a-tidal-wave-of-data/_jcr_content/par/articledownloadcompo/file.res/3897.Digital_Ocean_web.pdf, Accessed: 16 November 2014.

Doctorow, C. (2008). *Giving it Away*, pp. 71–75. Tachyon Publications, San Fransisco, CA, USA.

Doctorow, C. (2012a). *Lockdown: The Coming War on General-purpose Computing*. Boing Boing, 10 January 2012, boingboing.net/2012/01/10/lockdown.html, Accessed: January 2016.

Doctorow, C. (2012b). *Pirate Cinema*. Macmillan, London, England.

Doctorow, C. (2014). *Information Doesn't Want to Be Free: Laws for the Internet Age.* McSweeney's, San Francisco, CA, USA.

Dodd, T. (2015a). 'Coursera sets sights on universities'. *The Australian Financial Review,* 2 February 2015, afr.com/news/policy/education/coursera-sets-sights-on-universities-20150201-133fi5, Accessed: 27 December 2015.

Dodd, T. (2015b). 'University of Adelaide is phasing out lectures'. *The Australian Financial Review,* 28 June 2015, afr.com/technology/apps/education/university-of-adelaide-is-phasing-out-lectures-20150625-ghxgoz, Accessed: 27 December 2015.

Downes, S. and G. Siemens (2008). '03. CCK08 – The Distributed Course'. sites.google.com/site/themoocguide/3-cck08—the-distributed-course, Accessed: 26 December 2015.

Duncan, J. (1911). 'Efficiency – real, unreal, and brutal'. *American Federationist,* pp. 380–384.

Ebbeler, J. (2013). 'Intro chemistry class shows benefits of peer mentoring, online content'. *The Daily Texan,* 8 October 2013, dailytexanonline.com/opinion/2013/10/08/intro-chemistry-class-shows-benefits-of-peer-mentoring-online-content, Accessed: 27 December 2015.

Edwards, R. and D. Shulenburger (2003). 'The high cost of scholarly journals: (and what to do about it)'. *Change: The Magazine of Higher Learning* **35**(6):10–19.

EFF (2011a). *Princeton Scientists Sue Over Squelched Research.* Electronic Frontier Foundation. 6 June 2001, eff.org/press/releases/princeton-scientists-sue-oversquelched-research, Accessed: 2 January 2016.

EFF (2011b). *US v. ElcomSoft & Sklyarov FAQ.* Electronic Frontier Foundation. 19 February 2002, eff.org/pages/us-v-elcomsoft-sklyarov-faq, Accessed: 2 January 2016.

Enyedy, N. (2014). 'Personalized instruction: new interest, old rhetoric, limited results, and the need for a new direction for computer-mediated learning'. nepc.colorado.edu/publication/personalized-instruction, Accessed: 25 December 2015.

Eron, D. (2015). 'Professor Salaita's Intramural Speech'. *AAUP Journal of Academic Freedom* **6**:1–9.

Eveleth, R. (2014). 'Academics write papers arguing over how many people read (and cite) their papers'. *Smithsonian,* 25 March 2014, smithsonianmag.com/smart-news/half-academic-studies-are-never-read-more-three-people-180950222/?no-ist, Accessed: 28 December 2015.

Fain, P. (2014). 'Experimenting with aid'. *Inside Higher Education,* 23 July 2014, insidehighered.com/news/2014/07/23/competency-based-education-gets-boost-education-department, Accessed: 27 December 2015.

fedupatwgu (2012). *Why I'm here.* Fed up at WGU. 19 January 2012, fedupatwgu.wordpress.com/2012/01/19/hello-world/, Accessed: 27 December 2015.

Feldstein, M. (2014). *Pearson, Efficacy, and Research.* e-Literate. 1 December 2014, mfeldstein.com/pearson-efficacy-research/, Accessed: 25 December 2015.

Ferster, B. (2014). *Teaching Machines: Learning from the Intersection of Education and Technology.* Tech.edu: A Hopkins Series on Education and Technology. Johns Hopkins University Press, Baltimore, MD, USA.

Yahoo Finance. 'Stock tracking pages for Facebook, Inc., and Alphabet, Inc.'. finance.yahoo.com/q?s=Fb and finance.yahoo.com/q?s=Goog, Accessed: 29 October 2015.

Finn, J. D. (2002). 'Small classes in American schools: Research, practice, and politics'. *Phi Delta Kappan* **83**(7):551–560.

Fish, S. (2014). *Versions of Academic Freedom: From Professionalism to Revolution.* University of Chicago Press, Chicago, IL, USA.

Fletcher, S. (2013). 'How big data is taking teachers out of the lecturing business'. *Scientific American* **309**(2). scientificamerican.com/article/how-big-data-taking-teachers-out-of-lecturing-business/.

Foundation for Individual Rights in Education (2014). University of Kansas: Anti-NRA Tweet Results In Professor's Suspension. thefire.org/cases/university-of-kansas-anti-nra-tweet-results-in-professors-suspension/, Accessed: 28 December 2015.

Ford, M. (2015). *Rise of the Robots: Technology and the Threat of a Jobless Future.* NY: Basic Books.

Freeman, L. A. (2015). 'Instructor time requirements to develop and teach online courses'. *Online Journal of Distance Learning Administration* **18**(1). Spring 2015, westga.edu/ distance/ ojdla/spring181/freeman181.html, Accessed: 25 December 2015.

Friedman, M. (1970). 'A Friedman doctrine – the social responsibility of business is to increase its profits'. *New York Times,* 13 September 1970, timesmachine.nytimes.com/ timesmachine/1970/09/13/223535702.html, Accessed: 20 December 2015.

Friedman, T. (2012). 'Come the revolution'. *The New York Times,* 15 May 2012, nytimes. com/2012/05/16/opinion/friedman-come-the-revolution.html, Accessed: 26 December 2015.

Garber, A. M. (2015). 'Everywhere and anytime, here and now: digital and residential education at Harvard'. 13 October 2015, provost.harvard.edu/files/provost/files/online_ learning_whitepaper_final.pdf, Accessed: 26 December 2015.

Goldin, C. D. and L. F. Katz (2009). *The Race between Education and Technology.* Harvard University Press, Cambridge, MA, USA.

Google, Inc. (2015). 'A year in search'. google.com/trends/2014/, Accessed: 18 October 2015.

Greewald, G. (2013). 'The crux of the NSA story in one phrase: "collect it all"'. *The Guardian* 15 July 2013, theguardian.com/commentisfree/2013/jul/15/crux-nsa-collect-it-all, Accessed: 26 January 2016.

Haber, J. (2014). *MOOCs.* MIT Press, Cambridge, MA, USA.

Harris, K. D. (2013). *MOOC me.* Fair Matter Blog. 19 March 2013, fairmatter.com/ post/46596584975/mooc-me, Accessed: 27 December 2015.

Hartz, G. (2012). 'Why I changed my mind about teaching online'. *Chronicle of Higher Education,* 1 October 2012, chronicle.com/article/Why-I-Changed-My-Mind-About/134674/.

Haynie, D. (2014). 'What online students need to know about automated grading'. *US News & World Report,* 13 June 2014, usnews.com/education/online-education/articles/ 2014/06/13/what-online-students-need-to-know-about-automated-grading, Accessed: 26 December 2015.

Head, K. (2013a). 'Inside a MOOC in progress'. *The Chronicle of Higher Education,* 21 June 2013, chronicle.com/blogs/wiredcampus/inside-a-mooc-in-progress/44397, Accessed: 26 December 2015.

Head, K. (2013b). 'Sweating the details of a MOOC in progress'. *The Chronicle of Higher Education,* 3 April 2013, chronicle.com/blogs/wiredcampus/sweating-the-details-of-a-mooc-in-progress/43315, Accessed: 26 December 2015.

Hetter, K. (2015). *Online Fury over Boston University Professor's Tweets On Race.* CNN. 13 May 2015, cnn.com/2015/05/13/living/feat-boston-university-saida-grundy-race-tweets/index.html, Accessed: 28 December 2015.

Hilton III, J. and D. Wiley (2010). 'The short-term influence of free digital versions of books on print sales'. *Journal of Electronic Publishing* **14**(1). quod.lib.umich.edu/j/jep/3336451. 101?rgn=main;view=fulltext, Accessed: 31 December 2015.

Houghton, J. et al. (2009). 'Economic implications of alternative scholarly publishing models'. *A report to the Joint Information Systems Committee* vuir.vu.edu.au/15222/1/ EI-ASPM_Report.pdf, Accessed: 22 January 2016.

Hsu, J. (2012). *Professor Leaving Stanford for Online Education Startup.* Innovation on NBCNews. com. 25 January 2012, nbcnews.com/id/46138856/ns/technology_and_science-innovation/t/professor-leaving-stanford-online-education-startup/, Accessed: 26 December 2015.

Jacobs, A. (2013). 'Two cheers for Web U!' *New York Times* 20 April 2013, nytimes. com/2013/04/21/opinion/sunday/grading-the-mooc-university.html, Accessed: 26 December 2015.

Jaschik, S. (2012). 'The e-mail trail at UVa'. *Inside Higher Education* 20 June 2012.

Jaschik, S. (2015). 'Not a tsunami, but...'. *Inside Higher Education* 16 March 2015, insidehigh-ered.com/news/2015/03/16/stanford-president-offers-predictions-more-digital-future-higher-education, Accessed: 25 December 2015.

Kant, I. (1784). 'Beantwortung der Frage: Was is Aufklärung?' *Berlinische Monatschrift* **12**: 481–494.

Klapdor, T. (2015). *Social Media: A Story of Exploitation, Enclosure and Enslavement.* Heart—Soul—Machine. 26 November 2015, timklapdor.wordpress.com/2015/11/26/social-media-a-story-of-exploitation-enclosure-and-enslavement/, Accessed: 28 December 2015.

Kolowich, S. (2013a). 'The professors behind the MOOC hype'. *The Chronicle of Higher Education,* 18 March 2013, chronicle.com/article/The-Professors-Behind-the-MOOC/137905, Accessed: 26 December 2015.

Kolowich, S. (2013b). 'Why professors at San Jose State won't use a Harvard professor's MOOC'. *The Chronicle of Higher Education,* 2 May 2013, chronicle.com/article/Professors-at-San-Jose-State/138941, Accessed: 26 December 2015.

Kolowich, S. (2013c). 'Why some colleges are saying no to MOOC deals, at least for now'. *The Chronicle of Higher Education,* 20 April 2013, chronicle.com/article/Why-Some-Colleges-Are-Saying/138863, Accessed: 26 December 2015.

Kolowich, S. (2014). 'Writing instructor, skeptical of automated grading, pits machine vs. machine'. *The Chronicle of Higher Education,* 28 April 2014, chronicle.com/article/Writing-Instructor-Skeptical/146211/, Accessed: 26 December 2015.

Kolowich, S. (2015). 'When your online course is put up for adoption'. *The Chronicle of Higher Education,* 19 May 2015, chronicle.com/blogs/wiredcampus/when-your-online-course-is-put-up-for-adoption/56723, Accessed: 25 December 2015.

Koseff, A. (2014). *Capitol Alert: AM Alert: Jerry Brown Pushes UC To Find 'Outer Limits' Of Online Education.* Sacramento Bee, 23 January 2014, blogs.sacbee.com/capitolalertlatest/2014/01/am-alert-302.html, Accessed: 24 May 2015.

Krueger, A. B. (2003). 'Economic considerations and class size'. *The Economic Journal* **113**(485):F34–F63.

Lane, L. (2013). *On Being Orson.* Lisa's (Online) Teaching & History Blog. 13 July 2013, lisahistory.net/wordpress/2013/07/on-being-orson/, Accessed: 25 December 2015.

La Rue, F. (2011). *Report of the Special Rapporteur on the Promotion and Protection of the Right to Freedom of Opinion and Expression.* United Nations, 16 May 2011, U.N. Doc !/HRC/17/27, www2.ohchr.org/english/bodies/hrcouncil/docs/17session/A.HRC.17.27_en.pdf, Accessed: 17 Jan 2016.

Leckart, S. (2012). 'The Stanford education experiment could change higher learning for-ever'. *Wired Magazine* **20**. wired.com/2012/03/ff_aiclass/all/1, Accessed: 20 April 2014.

Ledford, H. (2013). 'Universities struggle to make patents pay'. *Nature* **501**:471–472, 26 September 2013, nature.com/news/universities-struggle-to-make-patents-pay=1.13811, Accessed: 30 December 2015.

Lehrer, T. (1965). 'New Math'. In *That Was the Year That Was.* Reprise/Warner Bros. Records.

Lenin, V. (1972). 'The immediate tasks of the Soviet Government'. In Lenin's *Collected Works,* 4th English edition, vol. 27, pp. 235–277. transl. Clemens Dutt, first published 28 April 1918 in *Pravda No. 83.*

Lenin, V. (1975). 'A "scientific" system of sweating'. In Lenin's *Collected Works*, 4th English edition, vol. 18, pp. 594–595. transl. Stepan Apresyan, first published 13 March 1913 in *Pravda No. 60*.

Lewin, T. (2011). 'Weekly prompts from a mentor'. *New York Times,* 25 August 2011, nytimes.com/2011/08/25/education/25future_WGU.html, Accessed: 27 December 2015.

Lieberman, M. B. and D. B. Montgomery (1988). 'First-mover advantages'. *Strategic Management Journal* **9**(1):41–58.

Lockhart, P. (2009). *A Mathematician's Lament*. Bellevue Literary Press, New York, NY, USA.

Madsen-Brooks, L. (2013). *True Innovation in Higher Ed Will Emerge From Faculty-Driven, Open-Source Projects, Not Start-Up Commercialisation*. LSE Impact Blog. 15 May 2013, blogs.lse.ac.uk/impactofsocialsciences/2013/05/15/beyond-disruption/, Accessed: 25 December 2015.

Markoff, J. (2013). 'Essay-grading software offers professors a break'. *New York Times,* 4 April 2013, nytimes.com/2013/04/05/science/new-test-for-computers-grading-essays-at-college-level.html, Accessed: 14 August 2015.

Markoff, J. (2015). *Machines of Loving Grace: The Quest for Common Ground Between Humans and Robots*. Ecco, New York, NY, USA.

Meinrath, S. (2013). 'We can't let the Internet become Balkanized'. *Slate* 14 October 2013, slate.com/articles/technology/future_tense/2013/10/internet_balkanization_may_be_a_side_effect_of_the_snowden_surveillance.html, Accessed: 25 January 2016.

Merkle, J. A. (1980). *Management and Ideology: The Legacy of the International Scientific Management Movement*. University of California Press, Berkeley, California.

Mintz, S. (2015). 'MOOC providers'. *Inside Higher Education, Higher Ed Beta* 16 August 2015, insidehighered.com/blogs/higher-ed-beta/mooc-providers, Accessed: 27 December 2015.

Moglen, E. (2012). *Innovation under Austerity*. Software Freedom Law Center. Transcript of a speech at the 2012 Freedom to Connect conference, 22 May 2012, softwarefreedom.org/events/2012/freedom-to-connect_moglen-keynote-2012.html, Accessed: 21 January 2016.

Moran, H. (2012). 'Online learning now essential, speakers say'. *Daily Titan,* 30 April 2012, dailytitan.com/2012/04/online-learning-now-essential-speakers-say/, Accessed: 25 December 2015.

Morris, E. (2011). 'The ashtray: Hippasus of Metapontum (Part 3)'. *The New York Times* 8 March 2011, opinionator.blogs.nytimes.com/2011/03/08/the-ashtray-hippasus-of-metapontum-part-3, Accessed: 10 January 2016.

NACS (2015). *Higher Education Retail Market Facts & Figures*. National Association of College Stores. nacs.org/research/industrystatistics/higheredfactsfigures.aspx, Accessed: 23 January 2016.

Noble, D. F. (2002). *Digital Diploma Mills: The Automation of Higher Education*. Monthly Review Press, New York, NY, USA.

Norman, M. (2014). 'Letting faculty drive'. *Inside Higher Education,* 21 November 2014, insidehighered.com/views/2014/11/21/faculty-members-must-own-online-learning-process-essay, Accessed: 23 July 2015.

Oden, L. (2015). 'Protecting yourself on social media, Part 1'. *Inside Higher Education, gradhacker,* 19 November 2015, insidehighered.com/blogs/gradhacker/protecting-yourself-social-media-part-1, Accessed: 28 December 2015.

Odlyzko, A. M. (1995). 'Tragic loss or good riddance? The impending demise of traditional scholarly journals'. *International Journal of Human-computer Studies* **42**(1):71–122.

Ota, A. K. (1998). 'Disney in Washington: The mouse that roars'. *Congressional Quarterly*, 10 August 1998, cnn.com/ALLPOLITICS/1998/08/10/cq/disney.html, Accessed: 1 January 2016.

Palmer, A. (2014). *The Art of Asking: How I Learned to Stop Worrying and Let People Help*. Hachette, London, England.

Palumbo-Liu, D. (2014). 'Return of the blacklist? Cowardice and censorship at the University of Illinois'. *Salon*, 7 August 2014, salon.com/2014/08/07/return_of_the_blacklist_cowardice_and_censorship_at_the_university_of_illinois/, Accessed: 28 December 2015.

Palumbo-Liu, D. (2015). 'Vindication for Steven Salaita: A victory for academic freedom in a textbook case of "the Israel exception"'. *Salon*, 14 November 2015, salon.com/2015/11/14/vindication_for_steven_salaita_a_victory_for_academic_freedom_in_a_textbook_case_of_the_israel_exception/, Accessed: 28 December 2015.

Pappano, L. (2012). 'The year of the MOOC'. *The New York Times*, 2 November 2012, nytimes.com/2012/11/04/education/edlife/massive-open-online-courses-are-multi-plying-at-a-rapid-pace.html, Accessed: 26 December 2015.

Parr, C. (2013). 'Not staying the course'. *Inside Higher Education*, 10 May 2013, insidehigh-ered.com/news/2013/05/10/new-study-low-mooc-completion-rates, Accessed: 26 December 2015.

Parry, M. (2013). 'A star MOOC Professor defects at least for now'. *The Chronicle of Higher Education* **60**(1).

Patry, W. (2009). *Moral Panics and the Copyright Wars*. Oxford University Press, Oxford, England.

Patry, W. (2012). *How to Fix Copyright*. Oxford University Press, Oxford, England.

Pauli, M. (2009). 'Making a revolution with Cory Doctorow'. *The Guardian*, 7 December 2009, theguardian.com/books/2009/dec/07/cory-doctorow-makers-interview, Accessed: 10 January 2016.

Pavlich, K. (2012). 'Professor: I want NRA Vice President's "head on a stick,"'. *Townhall* 18 December 2012, townhall.com/tipsheet/katiepavlich/2012/12/18/professor-i-want-nra-vice-presidents-head-on-a-stick-n1469395, Accessed: 28 December 2015.

Peekhaus, W. (2014). 'Digital content delivery in higher education: Expanded mechanisms for exploiting the professoriate and academic precariat'. *International Review of Information Ethics* **21**:57–63.

Perelman, G. (2002). 'The entropy formula for the Ricci flow and its geometric applications'. *arXiv.org preprint math/0211159*.

Perelman, G. (2003a). 'Finite extinction time for the solutions to the Ricci flow on certain three-manifolds'. *arXiv.org preprint math/0307245*.

Perelman, G. (2003b). 'Ricci flow with surgery on three-manifolds'. *arXiv.org preprint math/0303109*.

Perry, M. J. (2012). *The College Textbook Bubble and How The 'Open Educational Resources' Movement Is Going Up Against The Textbook Cartel*. Carpe Diem. 24 December 2012, aei.org/publication/the-college-textbook-bubble-and-how-the-open-educational-resources-movement-is-going-up-against-the-textbook-cartel, Accessed: 23 January 2016.

Pollan, M. (2013). *A Place of My Own: The Education of an Amateur Builder*. Random House, New York, NY, USA.

Popken, B. (2015). College Textbook Prices Have Risen 1,041 Percent Since 1977. *NBC News* 6 August 2015, nbcnews.com/feature/freshman-year/college-textbook-prices-have-risen-812-percent-1978-n399926, Accessed: 23 January 2015.

Poritz, J. A. (2014). *Yet Another Introductory Number Theory Textbook*. poritz.net/jonathan/share/yaintt/, Accessed: 16 January 2016.

PRN (2013). *Centenary College Sponsors New Online Global Database of Professors for Online Education*. PR NewsChannel. 24 June 2013, prnewschannel.com/2013/06/24/centenary-college-sponsors-new-online-global-database-of-professors/, Accessed: 25 December 2015.

Rankin, M. (2009). 'Some General Comments on "The Twitter Experiment"'. utdallas.edu/ mar046000/usweb/twitterconclusions.htm, Accessed: 28 December 2015.

Reed, M. (2015). 'Mystery solved?' *Inside Higher Education, Confessions of a Community College Dean,* 22 December 2015, insidehighered.com/blogs/confessions-community-college-dean/mystery-solved, Accessed: 20 January 2016.

Sandvine (2014). *Global Internet Phenomena Report*. sandvine.com/trends/global-internet-phenomena/, Accessed: 16 January 2016.

San Jose State University Philosophy Department (2013). *An Open Letter to Professor Michael Sandel from the Philosophy Department at San Jose State U., 29 April 2013*. 2 May 2013, chronicle.com/article/The-Document-an-Open-Letter/138937, Accessed: 26 December 2015.

Selingo, J. J. (2013). *College (Un)Bound: The Future of Higher Education and What It Means for Students*. Houghton Mifflin Harcourt, Boston, MA, USA.

Selingo, J. J. (2014). 'Demystifying the MOOC'. *The New York Times,* 29 October 2014, nytimes.com/2014/11/02/education/edlife/demystifying-the-mooc.html.

Senack, E. (2014). *Fixing the Broken Textbook Market: How Students Respond to High Textbook Costs and Demand Alternatives*. U.S. PIRG Education Fund & The Student PIRGs. uspirg.org/sites/pirg/files/reports/NATIONAL%20Fixing%20Broken%20Textbooks%20Report1.pdf, Accessed: 23 January 2016.

Shen, C. (2013). *Sebastian Thrun: Thoughts and Financial Transparency on our Masters in Computer Science with Georgia Tech*. 24 June 2013, blog.udacity.com/2013/06/sebastian-thrun-thoughts-and-financial.html, Accessed: 26 December 2015.

Shirky, C. (2008). *Here Comes Everybody: The Power of Organizing Without Organization*. Penguin, New York, NY, USA.

Shirky, C. (2015). *The Digital Revolution In Higher Education Has Already Happened. No One Noticed*. Medium. 6 November 2015, medium.com/@cshirky/the-digital-revolution-in-higher-education-has-already-happened-no-one-noticed-78ec0fec16c7#.w4lnul8tx, Accessed: 25 December 2015.

Silbey, J. (2014). *The Eureka Myth: Creators, Innovators, and Everyday Intellectual Property*. Stanford University Press, Redwood City, CA, USA.

Simon, S. (2015). *No Profit Left Behind*. Politico. 10 February 2015, politico.com/story/2015/02/pearson-education-115026.html, Accessed: 25 December 2015.

Smith, K. (2009). *The Twitter Experiment – Twitter in the Classroom*. Posted 2 May 2009, youtu.be/6WPVWDkF7U8, Accessed: 28 December 2015.

Stallman, R. M. et al. (2002). *Free Software, Free Society: Selected Essays of Richard M. Stallman*. Free Software Foundation, Boston, MA, USA.

Stewart, B. E. (2015). 'In abundance: Networked participatory practices as scholarship'. *The International Review of Research in Open and Distributed Learning* **16**(3). irrodl.org/index.php/irrodl/article/view/2158/3343, Accessed: 28 December 2015.

Stout, L. A. (2008). 'Why we should stop teaching Dodge v. Ford'. *Va. L. & Bus. Rev.* **3**:163.

Straumsheim, C. (2015a). 'Less than 1%'. *Inside Higher Education,* 21 December 2015, insidehighered.com/news/2015/12/21/323-learners-eligible-credit-moocs-arizona-state-u, Accessed: 20 Jan 2016.

Straumsheim, C. (2015b). 'We all felt trapped'. *Inside Higher Education* 23 January 2015, insidehighered.com/news/2015/01/23/complainant-unprecedented-walter-lewin-sexual-harassment-case-comes-forward, Accessed: 26 December 2015.

Suber, P. (2004). 'A very brief introduction to open access'. *On Peter Suber's website, earlham. edu/peters/fos/brief.htm, Accessed: 23 January 2016* released under a Creative Commons Attribution 3.0 United States License, creativecommons.org/licenses/by/3.0/us/.

Suber, P. (2012). *Open Access.* MIT Press Essential Knowledge. MIT Press, Cambridge, MA, USA. Freely available at bit.ly/oa-book.

Suber, P. (2015). 'Open access overview'. *On Peter Suber's website, earlham.edu/peters/fos/ overview.htm, Accessed: 22 January 2016* released under a Creative Commons Attribution 3.0 United States License, creativecommons.org/licenses/by/3.0/us/.

Summers, J. (2014). *Educators Not Satisfied With Revised Social Media Policy.* National Public Radio. 26 May 2014, npr.org/sections/ed/2014/05/25/315837245/educators-not-satis-fied-with-revised-kansas-social-media-policy, Accessed: 28 December 2015.

Suster, M. (2013). *In 15 Years from Now Half of US Universities May Be in Bankruptcy. My Surprise Discussion with Clay Christensen.* Both Sides of the Table. bothsidesofthetable. com/2013/03/03/in-15-years-from-now-half-of-us-universities-may-be-in-bank-ruptcy-my-surprise-discussion-with-claychristensen/, Accessed: 23 May 2015.

Swartz, A. (2016). *The Boy Who Could Change the World: The Writings of Aaron Swartz.* The New Press, New York, NY, USA.

Taylor F. W. (1914). *The Principles of Scientific Management.* Harper, New York, NY, USA.

Taylor, P. et al. (2011). *Is College Worth It?* Pew Research Center. 16 May 2011, pewsocial-trends.org/files/2011/05/higher-ed-report.pdf, Accessed: 23 May 2015.

Thomsen, J. (2015). 'In the mind of the student'. *Inside Higher Education* 25 September 2015, insidehighered.com/news/2015/09/25/researchers-uw-madison-hope-their-work-will-optimize-teachers-time-students, Accessed: 25 December 2015.

Tiede, H. J. (2015). *University Reform: The Founding of the American Association of University Professors.* The Johns Hopkins University Press, Baltimore, MD, USA.

Tracey, N. (2013). *Harmony and Discord in Berklee's Songwriting MOOC.* 3 July 2013, mooc-newsandreviews.com/harmony-and-discord-berklees-songwriting-mooc/, Accessed: 26 December 2015.

Turing, A. M. (1950). 'Computing machinery and intelligence'. *Mind* pp. 433–460.

Turkle, S. (2011). *Alone Together: Why We Expect More from Technology and Less from Each Other.* Basic Books, New York, NY, USA.

Vanden Bout, D. et al. (2013). *Chemistry 301 Syllabus.* ctp.cm.utexas.edu/courses/fall2013/ch301/syllabus.php, Accessed: 27 December 2015.

Warner, J. (2014). 'ASU English by the numbers: It ain't pretty'. *Just Visiting, Inside Higher Ed,* 18 December 2014, insidehighered.com/blogs/just-visiting/asu-english-numbers-it-aint-pretty, Accessed: 24 May 2015.

Watters, A. (2014a). *Top Ed-Tech Trends 2014: Data and Privacy.* Hack Education. 15 December 2014, 2014trends.hackeducation.com/data.html, Accessed: 25 December 2015.

Watters, A. (2014b). '[Tweet]'. 11 December 2014, twitter.com/audreywatters/status/543289782197956608, Accessed: 24 May 2015.

Watters, A. and S. Goldrick-Rab (2015). 'Techno fantasies'. *Inside Higher Education,* 26 March 2015, insidehighered.com/views/2015/03/26/essay-challenging-kevin-careys-new-book-higher-education, Accessed: 25 December 2015.

Weller, M. (2015). *2016—the Year of MOOC Hard Questions.* The Ed Techie, 11 December 2015, blog.edtechie.net/mooc/2016-the-year-of-mooc-hard-questions, Accessed: 20 January 2016.

Wente, M. (2012). 'We're ripe for a great disruption in higher education'. *Globe and Mail,* 4 February 2012, theglobeandmail.com/globe-debate/were-ripe-for-a-great-disruption-in-higher-education/article543479/, Accessed: 27 December 2015.

Wexler, E. (2015). 'As Academia.edu grows, some scholars voice concerns'. *Chronicle of Higher Education,* 2 December 2015, chronicle.com/article/As-Academiaedu-Grows-Some/234414, Accessed: 28 December 2015.

Wheeler, T. (2015). 'FCC Chairman Tom Wheeler: This is how we will ensure net neutrality'. *Wired Magazine,* 4 February 2015, wired.com/2015/02/fcc-chairman-wheeler-net-neutrality, Accessed: 21 January 2016.

Whythe, P. (2015). 'U. online facial recognition system presents major privacy risk'. *The Daily Targum,* 12 February 2015, dailytargum.com/article/2015/02/u-online-facial-recognition-system-presents-major-privacy-risk, Accessed: 25 December 2015.

Wiggins, B. (2014). *Can Peer Grading Actually Work?* More or Less Bunk, 17 February 2014, moreorlessbunk.wordpress.com/2014/02/17/can-peer-grading-actually-work/, Accessed: 26 December 2015.

Williams, J. J. (2014). 'The innovation agenda'. *Inside Higher Education,* 8 December 2014, insidehighered.com/views/2014/12/08/essay-way-higher-education-reformers-misunderstand-role-professors, Accessed: 25 December 2015.

Wilson, J. K. (2015). *On Extramural Utterances.* The Academe Blog, 23 September 2015, academeblog.org/2015/09/23/on-extramural-utterances/, Accessed: 28 December 2015.

Winerip, M. (2012). 'Facing a Robo-Grader? Just keep obfuscating mellifluously'. *New York Times,* 22 April 2012, nytimes.com/2012/04/23/education/robo-readers-used-to-grade-test-essays.html, Accessed: 27 December 2015.

Young, J. R. (2015). 'Many colleges now see centers for teaching with technology as part of "Innovation Infrastructure"'. *Chronicle of Higher Education Wired Campus,* 3 November 2015, chronicle.com/blogs/wiredcampus/many-colleges-now-see-centers-for-teaching-with-technology-as-part-of-innovation-infrastructure/57593, Accessed: 27 December 2015.

Zuckerberg, M. (2015). 'Post dated August 27, 2015'. facebook.com/zuck/posts/10102329188394581, Accessed: 18 October 2015.

INDEX